"God is present in our world, awaiting with wings of love to infuse hope."

This Hope We Have

Selected Sermons and Meditations of JON APPLETON

© 2017

Published in the United States by Nurturing Faith Inc., Macon GA,

www.nurturingfaith.net.

Library of Congress Cataloging-in-Publication Data is available.

ISBN 978-1-63528-016-6

All rights reserved. Printed in the United States of America.

Cover photo by David Cassady, Faithlab.

This book of selected sermons and meditations is published through the generosity of the family of Jon Appleton (1934–2016) and dedicated to his loving memory.

Oh, the joy—
of anticipation,
of experience,
of memory.

—Jon Appleton, 1990

Table of Contents

Foreword by Catherine Appleton Peay vii

Preface by John D. Pierce ix

Sermons for Hopeful Living...1
  Looking for Jesus *Genesis 12:1-7; Luke 24:1-7, 28-35*............... 2
  When Death Comes *2 Corinthians 4:16–5:10* 4
  Forgiveness *Isaiah 53:10-12; Luke 23:32-38*................................. 7
  Jesus and Integrity *Matthew 4:18-22* 10
  Acting Medium *Romans 12:1-21* 13
  Religion Is a Verb *Deuteronomy 30:15-20; 1 John 4:21*............ 16
  The Talent(s) Tally *Matthew 25:14-30* 19
  We Have Good News to Share *Matthew 5:16* 22
  The Bible: God's Story *2 Timothy 3:16-17; 2 Peter 2:20-21*.......... 24
  Overcoming Our Timidity *Matthew 25:14-30* 27
  God's Call *Genesis 12:1-4a*.. 30

Sermons from the Gospel of John 33
  Jesus' First Sign *John 2:1-11*.. 34
  The Angry Jesus *John 2:13-17*.. 37
  The Father and the Son *John 5:19-20, 30* 40
  Mercy *John 8:1-11* 43
  To See or Not to See *John 9*.. 47
  Unbind Him! Let Him Go! *John 11:38-44* 51
  On Being Extravagant *John 12:1-8* 53

Sermons for Special Occasions 57
  Deacons: Do You, Therefore? *2 Timothy 2:15* 58
  Epiphany: Time-conscious *Ecclesiastes 3:1-11* 60
  Father's Day: Models of Love *Isaiah 41:4c, 6-7, 10b, 17, 20* 63
  Mother's Day: About Relationships *Psalm 139*........................... 66
  Not Just Thanks-giving, but Thanks-living *John 14:15-31* 69

Sermons for Advent and Christmas 71
   Resounding Hope *1 Thessalonians 3:1-13*... 72
   Jesus Christ: Light and Life *John 1:1-18*.. 75
   Upon Being Ready *Matthew 24:36-44*... 77
   John, the Forerunner *Luke 3:1-20* 79
   Wonder, Ponder, and Adore *Luke 2:1-20*... 82
   God Is with Us *Matthew 1:18-25* 85
   Christmas Eve: A Poem 87
   Tomorrow! Oh, Tomorrow *Isaiah 35:1-10*... 88
   The Child, His Authority *Isaiah 9:2-7* 91
   Sacrifices, Gifts, and Presents *Luke 2:22-40; Romans 12:1-8* 93
   God's Boy and Bess, Oh Bess *John 1:14* 96

Communion Meditations 99
   Freed from Hiding *Isaiah 50:4-9*.. 100
   Washing Another's Feet *John 13:1-17* 101
   The Best Is Yet To Be *John 2:1-11*... 103
   Stretch Out Your Hand *John 6:35, 51b, 54*... 104
   Being One With Others *John 10:16*.. 106
   Three Acts *Matthew 4:19; 1 Corinthians 11:24; Acts 3:6* 107

Sermons for Holy Week and Easter 109
   "It Is Finished" *Psalm 22:27-31; John 19:28-30*.................................. 110
   To See Jesus *John 12:20-32*... 112
   Good Friday: To Despair *Matthew 27:45-46*...................................... 114
   The Resurrection Conspiracy *John 20:19-22*...................................... 117
   Resurrections: His and Ours *John 20:1-18*... 120
   "I Have Seen the Lord!" *John 20:1, 11-18* 122

A Pastoral Prayer... 125
   Thank You, Lord!... 126

Epilogue 127
   A Good Name and Loving Favor *Proverbs 22:1* 128
      by Paul A. Baxley

Benediction 133

Foreword

Sitting in the congregation, watching with pride as my father delivered his sermons, is a wonderful memory. Then it was absolutely exhilarating to go home with this much-admired man being my daddy.

Growing up the son of a Baptist minister, Jon Appleton was destined to follow in his father's footsteps. Of his calling he once wrote,

> As a young man sensing "a call" to ministry, little is perceived about "the bigness" of such a beckoning. Such naivety allows the possible rush of joy intermixed with wonder and humility to trust that "all things are possible; only believe." A part of working out one's calling is the daunting, compelling task of becoming one's self.

Jon Appleton worked diligently in studying and being mentored by those who helped him develop and define his life as a minister. He was ever evolving, feeling there were and always would be questions. He reveled in searching for answers.

Jon's sense of humor served him well. The devilish grin and look in his eyes were captivating to those with whom he came in contact. It was an endearing quality incorporated into his ministry.

In the pulpit he delivered heartfelt, thoughtful, and thought-provoking messages. His brief and to-the-point sermons were among his trademarks. Those in attendance would leave the services with smiles on their faces and something in their hearts to contemplate.

Jon loved people from all walks of life, accepting their right to view Scripture and life differently. He encouraged open dialogue and won many friends by listening without chastising.

Many would say you could look far and wide yet come up empty in finding a person whose charisma replicates that of Jon Appleton.

Our family's hope is that the sermons and meditations in this book will be inspirational and give a glimpse into the heart of the man who spoke this poetry of truth.

Catherine Appleton Peay
Highland, North Carolina

Preface

Jon Appleton's preaching notes were crafted for proclamation rather than publication. But, fortunately, they were preserved.

Some of his sermons were written in outline form—with phrases and single words to trigger Jon's mind—more so than as manuscripts. As for most preachers in the final stages of preparation before delivery, there are handwritten notes in the margins and changes to the typed text. These notations included self-reminders such as "tell the Alpine story." It is likely that Jon's beloved wife, Virginia, and some of the congregants in Athens, Georgia, could tell those stories, too.

Jon made good use of his multiple communication gifts. His sermons were a balanced blend of scholarship, humor, storytelling, poetry, and application.

Within the inspiring pages of this book are selected sermons, including several from Holy Week and Easter as well as from the Advent and Christmas seasons. Some of Jon's Communion meditations, a pastoral prayer, and a benediction are included as well.

Often, throughout the year, he would turn to his beloved Gospel of John for inspiration. Several of those sermons are compiled into this collection.

While Jon preached from a variety of texts and addressed many relevant topics for worship and Christian living, there is one common thread. Jon Appleton embraced and proclaimed hope—hence the title of this volume, *The Hope We Have*.

May those who read these collected words encounter—or encounter again—this great hope that Jon called "the cement of Christian commitment." Such "real hope," Jon proclaimed, is "the hope that God can do through us what we cannot do for ourselves."

Such hopeful words deserve proclamation and publication so they may be embraced again and again.

John D. Pierce
Editor/Publisher
Nurturing Faith

Sermons for Hopeful Living

"When all is said and done, our hope revolves around our God, who is a verb, and who will accept all of us into eternal fellowship, who are verbs."

—Jon Appleton, 1986

Looking for Jesus

Genesis 12:1-7; Luke 24:1-7, 28-35

Soon after the completion of Disney World, a tourist said, "Isn't it too bad that Walt Disney didn't live to see this?" Mark Vance, creative director of Disney Studios, replied, "He did see it; that's why it's here."

The writer of Hebrews said of Abraham: "By faith, Abraham obeyed when he was called to set out for a place that he was to receive as an inheritance; and he set out, not knowing where he was going" (11:8).

Abraham was not present on resurrection morning. But when he left Ur of the Chaldees, "not knowing where he was going," he possessed the eyes of faith, and resurrection morning was set.

When faith is a response to God's hints, everything that occurs thereafter is the fruit of believing in God's promptings. Abraham did not see his great-grandchildren, but because of his faithful eyes they became the twelve tribes of Israel.

Likewise, others had faithful eyes: Moses and the children of Israel leaving Egypt, striking out for the promised land; David and the loftiest heir of Israel's history; and Isaiah, whose faithful eyes beheld "a child" yet to be born.

Abraham was not in Bethlehem at the birth of Jesus or on the mount to hear Jesus teach. He was not at Golgotha when Jesus was on the cross or at the empty tomb to hear of the risen Christ.

Some might say, "Isn't it too bad that Abraham didn't live to see all these things?" However, when all these things (and much more) did occur, it is right to say, "He did see them; that's why they occurred." Had he not gone out, "not knowing where he was going," what did occur would not have occurred.

One of life's most gratifying yet most humbling realities is the significance that is attached to the faith we receive and the faith we impart.

There are those who look for God—God's hand, God's plan, God's hints—in wrong places. Take the two men on the road to Emmaus: They had been followers of Jesus objectively, but subjectively their expectations of him hindered their ability to perceive God's true call to them through Jesus. They heard Jesus teach about the kingdom of God, but in their minds such a kingdom was perceived as earthly—a military effort to restore Israel and to remove Rome. What Jesus said was colored by what they wanted him to say. Hearing *kingdom*, they thought *throne*. But in saying *kingdom*, Jesus was speaking of serving and a spiritual realm for all people. So when they learned about the empty tomb, they did not recall his words about rising on the third day. Rather, they assumed that thieves had stolen his body.

Those two on the road to Emmaus were so unlike Abraham, who believed in what God hinted, unreservedly. Before sunset they were intent upon getting home because they had not faithful eyes to see what they had been told. So they turned their backs on the empty tomb, thinking all was lost.

Our prayer, as modern believers, is that we might have faithful eyes, as Abraham did. He so believed in God's promises that he accepted, at a preposterous old age, the adventure into the unknown. He trusted in God, who called him. He believed in God, who would not have called him to an unknown destiny without God being a companion on the way, ready to fill in the gaps.

It does not take much imagination to assume that Abraham was ridiculed and laughed at by his contemporaries when they saw the Mayflower vans loading his belongings—headed toward an unknown residence. Later on that journey, his wife, Sarah, was to laugh when hearing that she and Abraham were to have a child—Abraham being 100 years old and she 90.

An indictment upon us may be that we practice a safe faith, we believe only as we see, and we allow little room for trust. God gives hints, but we overlook those clues.

God calls us to participate—revealing enough light, providing enough clues on the stage for us to react in faith's drama. Yet most of us hold back, waiting for God's dramatic moments. In doing so we miss out on being a participant with God. After all, we want to be safely home before dark—back to Emmaus.

The Bible is a story that covers hundreds of years. Yet there is a thread running through that story that says God does not want to be a soloist. God invites us to come along and sing along. God will announce the performance places as they occur. God will fill in the gaps.

In our looking for Jesus, one sign that we have indeed found him may well be that we have been laughed at because of our faith, trust, and belief; laughed at because of the way we sing. If we can recall being laughed at, then there is evidence we believe the mountains that "cannot" be climbed, *can* be climbed; the rivers that "cannot" be forded, *can* be forded; the deserts that "cannot" be crossed, *can* be crossed; the relationships that "cannot" be reclaimed, *can* be reclaimed; the sins that "cannot" be forgiven, *can* be forgiven.

So as we go "looking for Jesus," may we be as laughable as Abraham.

4/23/95

When Death Comes

2 Corinthians 4:16–5:10

Years ago in Opelika, Alabama, I was to conduct the funeral of a man I did not know. The man's son was a member of the church I served as pastor, so with that connection I was called upon to lead the graveside burial. The evening before the funeral I visited with the family.

It is not unusual for a minister to officiate at the burial of strangers, but I have always felt compelled to meet such a one as clearly as possible through surviving family members and friends. Often these postmortem introductions have led me to "know" the person over whom I would say last words.

It was to be a graveside service, I was told, and I assumed it would occur at the local cemetery, Memorial Garden, in Opelika. One quirk I have is arriving at meetings and/or speaking engagements in time to walk in, take my place, and get on with it. I think the service was scheduled for 2 p.m. Within five minutes of the hour, I calmly drove into Memorial Garden, looking for the telltale sign of a funeral tent.

About halfway into the cemetery, a strange feeling of panic ricocheted through my body. There was no tent! Frederick's Funeral Home was just down the road. As I left Memorial Garden, I did not do so calmly. I raced into the parking lot of the funeral home, leaped from the car, and burst into the secretary's office. She was as startled to see me as I was glad to see her. She shouted, "Why aren't you at Mt. Olive?" Without a single word of response, I was back in the car, speeding toward Mt. Olive, and it was 2:05 p.m.

Mt. Olive was a Primitive Baptist church in rural Lee County, some ten miles south of Opelika on a farm-to-market road. As I rounded the last curve, my heart, which had been racing faster than I drove, sank into my stomach. People were leaving the graveside, many already at their cars and all looking at me as I slid to a stop off the side of the pavement.

I remember dropping my head and thinking, "Lord, is there room in that coffin for me?" When I got out of my car, the man's son, Gene Ward, was walking toward me. Gene, who was county coroner, was a part-time employee at Frederick's Funeral Home. I began to ask for his forgiveness, but Gene held up his hand to stop me, and with a hint of a smile on his face, he said, "Jon, Reverend Summerall, an old family friend, was here, and he graciously volunteered to fill in. We weren't sure we should go on, but we finally agreed. It was brief, and he did a fine job, knowing Dad like he did. But halfway through Psalm 23 we knew you hadn't forgotten us. We heard you coming from at least three miles away."

Then he put his arm around my shoulders and walked me aside, whispering, "Jon, we'd gotten up a pool at the funeral home, a wager on whether or not you'd ever miss a service. Walter Jackson and I drew the tickets that said you would. After we split the pot, I'll net about thirty dollars. I always sorta figured you'd miss one—just didn't dream it would be my dad's service."

By ordinary expectant family reactions this was not an ordinary reaction. I have never forgotten my failure of duty or Gene's super acceptance of my loss of professionalism.

I made my way to apologize to the family and to thank Reverend Summerall. They were all very nice, but they did not look upon me as "minister of the year." I returned to my car and drove on out into the country, hoping to put myself back together again. Finally, I turned around and headed toward home.

As I neared Mt. Olive, everyone had gone. I drove into the churchyard and walked into the cemetery to Mr. Ward's plot. I stood a long time, looking at the freshly piled dirt and the many flowers. I reached into my coat pocket, took out my service book, read Psalm 1, and talked a bit to Mr. Ward and God. I told Mr. Ward how I wished I had known him, how I had messed up, and how he had a gracious wife, exceptional children (especially Gene), and many friends.

Then I told God how I was glad to know him and not to think he'd made a mistake in calling me to be a minister. I asked God not to take this lapse of duty as a sign that I didn't care about people, especially people in times of bereavement, suffering, and loss. As I turned to leave, my legs were not able to take my weight. I felt dizzy and stumbled toward a grave marker, where I took a seat. I have no idea how long I sat there.

Looking back, I couldn't have been more than twenty-eight or twenty-nine years old when this happened. It was one of those down, down times in my life; a time when I failed; a time when I let other people down; a time when I let God down. Something inside of me felt as dead as Mr. Ward. As death had come to his physical body, death was toying with my spirit.

Then I began to revive in that rural cemetery in a way that is still alive in me. I experienced from my depth of failure a resurrection. As I regained my legs and walked toward the car, I knew God (and even Mr. Ward) had somehow, someway reached down and removed the toying guilt of my failure.

I have never shared this whole story with anyone before. It was so personal, so calling, so real, and so private. One day, like Mr. Ward, we will all die. Death does come physically as mortals; that is our lot. But before that death there will be "little" deaths—not being present for responsibilities, not being present for a child's recital, not being present for a parent's birthday, not being present for worship. These "little" deaths inappropriately addressed can lead to withdrawal from life. These "little" deaths, which toy with our spirit, can cause us to get into our cars and drive out into a far country and never come back.

We are beset with "little" deaths as we fail in attentiveness, duty, and feeling. How easy it is when we do fail to give up, to secede, to run. Have we ever lied? Have we ever walked away from responsibilities? Ever cheated? Ever avoided encounter? Ever stolen? Ever disappeared when we were needed? Yes, and in so doing we did a "little" dying.

On the way back to town, I drove to the Wards' home. They were all there, drinking coffee and eating cake. I was invited in, and calling the whole family together, I requested a moment to do what they had asked me to do at the graveside.

A few times in my life I have really felt God's Spirit come upon a group of people. The Spirit came that day, and as I finished, tongues of fire fell on every member of the family as they each gave witness about the Lord, about Mr. Ward, and about how they loved and cherished one another.

When things settled down, Gene asked me what had happened to cause me to be late, so I told my story. Before telling my story, tears were in the eyes of everyone in that room; it had been that kind of drama. But as my story unfolded, smiles and then laughter erupted in the room. Again, I felt what I had felt at the cemetery: resurrection.

I could never undo my absence from Mr. Ward's graveside service with his family. That was gone—one of life's "little" deaths. But I was with his family at this moment when we were resurrected into what could have never happened between us at Mt. Olive Cemetery. We shared tears; we shared laughter.

When death comes, it is final. But in Christ there is resurrection. Death is cutting, but in Christ there is release. Death is lonely, but in Christ there is fellowship.

As I left, Mrs. Ward hugged me and with tears in her eyes and a smile on her face said, "Mr. Ward would have loved you!" I thanked her for the compliment, but inside I already knew how Mr. Ward felt about me.

2/25/90

Forgiveness

Isaiah 53:10-12; Luke 23:32-38

Life is the full story—and for many it is a long story before the sequence of chapters makes sense and provides meaning. For some, the meaning is heroic; for others, it is a tragedy.

For some, long years of guilt are overlaid by the ebb and flow of time. The echoes of sins past have a way of resounding at the junctures of memory and recall.

I heard of one who years ago cheated on his doctrinal dissertation, copying extended sections verbatim of an old thesis. He had bright promises of a career in academia, but the residents of academia knew that chapter in his story, and he never fulfilled other chapters as a result.

Many are the loopholes and politics in academia, but cheating is anathema. It is such a waste, such a burden, such a loss, such guilt to live a lifetime marred by a deed that need not have occurred. Shortcuts for vested interests that skip integrity, evade responsibility, and circumvent honor are fodder for guilt-ridden, sleepless nights and the tortures of memory.

Do you recall the remarkable story of Joseph in the Old Testament? Joseph's brothers had sold him into slavery and concocted a story for their father, claiming to have found his robe splattered with blood, indicating that he had been "torn to pieces" by a fierce beast. It was a terrible chapter in the story of Jacob's family.

For years, the story was not challenged, and Joseph's father never stopped grieving. His brothers could never blot out the memory of their act, the deception of their story, and the agony painted upon their father's face. Shortcuts for vested interests that skip integrity, evade responsibility, and circumvent honor are fodder for guilt-ridden, sleepless nights and the tortures of memory.

Joseph's brothers were out of sorts with Joseph and Jacob's bond of love and affection. These brothers, venting all their anger, were so wrought up over Joseph that their first choice was murder. Brother Reuben, however, persuaded them to throw him in a pit with the thought of rescuing him later. Then a caravan of Ishmaelites was spotted, and another brother, Judah, proposed the option of selling him for twenty pieces of silver.

It goes without saying that Jesus was a problem for the religious and political elite of his day. In time there were enough concern and consternation generated against him. When, finally, the arrangements to get rid of him were invoked, it was no ordinary band of malcontents who enacted the drama, orchestrated to be effective without a flaw. The powerful elite had enough cheek to move mountains overnight in corroboration with Judas, to get the ear of Pilate, to arrange an audience with Herod, to assemble a night court, and to incite the people to respond to Pilate's offer, screaming, "Crucify him! Crucify him!"

The charges brought against Jesus were, if anything, circumstantial, somewhat varied by strict religious orthodoxy, but not sufficient to merit a death sentence by Roman legal standards. Yet enough insinuation, enough whispering, enough hearsay, enough character assassination, enough betrayal, enough darkness, enough frustration ignited by a few intentional people, well-placed authoritatively, who possessed the means to get attention, and to incite questions, and to foster fear, and to mobilize a crowd, were able to bring about the sentence of crucifixion not only of an innocent man, but also the man who could do for all of them what each of them desperately needed and could not do for themselves.

Jesus' first words from the cross were a testimony to that reality: "Father, forgive them, for they do not know what they are doing" (Luke 23:34).

Vito, the puppeteer in James Michener's novel, *The Fires of Spring*, said, "Any life in the world, no matter how tangled or distressed, could be set free if only a friend would unravel the snarled strings." Otherwise, we miss the encompassing worth of the Christian faith in its character of forgiveness.

Jesus' word of forgiveness resounds from the cross toward those who had placed him there, toward those on the crosses adjacent to him, and toward us today. This is a most significant chapter in the story of Jesus. His forgiving word from the cross reveals a love without limit, a grace amid chaos, and a power beyond defeat.

Do you recall the end of Joseph's story? Joseph becomes the most powerful authority in Egypt with his brothers kneeling in submission, awaiting the final chapter in their long, agonizing story. And Joseph says, "I forgive you. What you meant as evil [and it was evil], God has turned into good."

Jesus from his cross prayed to God, "Father, forgive them; they know not what they do!" So was every guilty person, in a moment, made lily pure? I don't know how to answer that question.

Edna McDonagh reminds us, "Forgiveness opens the doors of possibility, provided it is accompanied as always by repentance." The way of forgiveness is the character of God, but it is only available to a repentant heart.

There is no way to account for the acceptance of Jesus' word of forgiveness for all who were guilty for his being on the cross. But I do know that at least one person heard him and asked for his mercy, and Jesus promised him that he would share with him, that very day, a place in paradise.

This very moment we leap through the centuries since Jesus spoke his word of forgiveness from the cross. There is a sense in which that past moment is always a present moment.

Jesus hangs ever because of sin, past and present. But the countershock of the first word from the cross is a plea of the one dying, not to charge anyone with the offense.

His crucifixion occurred 2,000 years ago, but it is happening even now. Yet he prays, "Forgive them." And how could anyone refuse so great an offer?

3/26/95

Jesus and Integrity

Matthew 4:18-22

Starting out in life is a challenge. What are my strengths, weaknesses, interests, and concerns? Will what I become bring satisfaction? Will the compensation be worthwhile for me, for my family, for others? Will what I do open doors for my faith to grow? Will what I do be pleasing in the sight of God?

As these challenges confront us, even so Jesus was challenged when he changed careers at thirty years of age. It is noteworthy that he chose to begin on such a "low key."

Because of who he was, he could have been a spellbinder, fashioning a display to nod and to win the acclaim of the multitudes. However, even when circumstances arose in which he did respond miraculously, he often drew aside quickly, asking that it not be mentioned what he did. Perhaps it was his encounter with Satan in the wilderness that led him to begin without fanfare.

Looking closely at the Gospel parallels, we note that Jesus began his ministry near the Sea of Galilee, in the villages and the fields adjacent to the Galilean Heights, choosing to associate with rather ordinary people like fishermen and even controversial ones like a tax collector. We find him moving about—avoiding concentration in one locale and at times fleeing from the multitudes.

Perhaps during the start of his new career, he did make a journey to Jerusalem, but his stay was brief, and he soon returned to Galilee. His had not emerged as a household name. Those whom he touched and taught, without doubt, began to question his identity (his profession), yet even in his hometown he was recognized only as Joseph's son, not the long-awaited Messiah.

We know him so well that we assume he was well known throughout Palestine, from his baptism to his ascension. However, the Bible reveals that the first year he worked to build a foundation, selectively choosing a few disciples whom he taught intentionally and primarily privately about the long road ahead. It is correct to say that he began in obscurity. In time multitudes came seeking him, but initially he took it upon himself to seek his followers.

Rudyard Kipling, on the eastern shore of India, wrote that "the sun comes up like thunder out of China cross the bay." But not so with Jesus—"the light of the world"—who came quietly, unpretentiously. Though his moves were cautious, some significant work occurred, such as his penetrating call to an inquirer: "Let the dead bury the dead and come and follow me."

Jesus' call, then and now, remains the same: "If anyone would come after me, let him/her deny self and take up his/her cross and follow me." With absolute integrity and bold honesty, these two simple words of invitation ("follow me") cut through a maze of theology, bowing neither to rank nor privilege. That clarion call, voiced 2,000 years ago, has an echo today that individuals find affirming, audacious, risky, and fulfilling.

Jesus was going someplace. The comfort of hibernation is a faith-killing virus. We have great proficiency in "holing up" in the comfort zones of dens or workrooms, verifying the benign hobbies that give us a sense of importance while allowing us to opt out on adventure, daring, and risk.

We find laughter in the t-shirt that reads, "Don't Follow Me; I'm Lost!" But the voice of Jesus asserts, "Follow me!"—and it is no laughing matter. The root of the word *follow* in the New Testament is the Greek word for *road*. To follow is to share the same road, with an avowed intent to purposively be in step. And Jesus was going someplace.

Those who follow will find themselves in places they would not have known to go without being in the footsteps of Jesus. His invitation had a futuristic design. Where the future portends uncertainty, fear, and trepidation, Jesus replaces anxiety with a steadfast trust.

However, many of us cannot turn toward the future with hope because we are burdened by yesterday's failures. With the call of Jesus, it's not where we've been that matters but where we are going; it's not whether we have fallen but whether we'll get up. Too many of us rummage around in the past, digging up reasons why we cannot take the steps and the leaps of faith. Some of us are held prisoner not by others but by our own sense of inadequacy due to past mistakes, failures, and defeats.

Read through the Gospels. You will be startled to discover how little time Jesus spent allowing people to expand on a burdened past. The examples are many:

- The woman taken in adultery, for whom Jesus did not require a case study: He simply took her hand and said, "Go your way, and sin no more" (John 5:11).
- Nicodemus—shackled by an impossible legalism—came by night to Jesus, who did not condemn him but said simply, "You must be born from above" (John 3:3).

- The prodigal son, who planned a speech but was not given room to recite it: His would-be confession was smothered in his father's love and rejoicing (Luke 15).

Jesus had about him a way for people to find hope rather than be swamped in despair. He offered trust rather than guilt and assurance rather than doubt. Jesus turns us toward the future.

Jesus becomes the follower's example. He does not absorb us into his being to become spiritual robots. Rather, he honors our selfhood, giving us leverage for our own integrity. He calls us to follow him, knowing it will be a struggle for us to keep in step. This is true of us individually; it is likewise true for the church.

An abiding concern for those of us who have said "Yes, I'll follow!" is to take note of where we are, to make sure we are on the path our Master walks.

Those who were captivated by Jesus and his integrity—and have said "Yes, I'll follow!"—moved from their chosen ways onto the path he led. And it made all the difference in the world.

The poet Robert Frost famously spoke of taking the road "less traveled." However, the path of Jesus, though demanding, really does make all the difference. So it was! So it can be!

6/4/95

Acting Medium

Romans 12:1-21

Some neighborhood children got together, collected large cardboard boxes, and worked diligently and creatively in building a clubhouse. Upon completion they gathered to decide upon the rules for club membership:

1. Nobody act big.
2. Nobody act small.
3. Everybody act medium.

The Olympics portray "big" people, whose strength and/or endurance allow them to win gold. However, if you were to go back with them through the formative days of training, the rigors of their discipline, and the sacrificial demands they imposed upon themselves, you would find from most of them devotion and commitment to simply doing ordinary things in an extraordinary manner.

Muhammad Ali, during his reign as heavyweight boxing champion, was one of those "big" people who would not have been fit for membership in the children's club, especially after he gave himself the title "The Greatest." During that era of greatness, he was traveling one day on an airplane. As it was taxying toward takeoff, a flight attendant admonished him to buckle his seatbelt. "Superman don't need to buckle up," he told her. The flight attendant responded, "Superman don't need an airplane."

Don't we usually find that people who suppose themselves to be "big"—important, noteworthy—lack the experience to understand that their significance and place are bestowed upon them by a grace not of their devise? Rather, it is by the circumstances of many others who believed in them, opened doors for them, and kept their attention on their endeavors. We appreciate and are awed by "bigness" more when its expression is not by show or ostentation but rather by its obvious presence and reality.

I like the children's rule: Nobody act big. However, there are those at the opposite pole who thrive on acting "small."

Thomas Tewell, pastor of the Fifth Avenue Presbyterian Church in New York City, refers to such people as "the cobweb spotters." Their delight is in pointing out the little things in relation to big things—that for them diminish the significance of the whole. Those whose time is spent highlighting the cobwebs are drawing attention to the obscure, probably because of their own lack of neatness, precision, and decisiveness—all lacking self-esteem.

In the real world "small" people also lack maturity to see that even when flaws are evident in a person, a plan, or a program, it does not mean that the person is not right for the position, or the plan is not worthy of enacting, or a program is not substantive for support. Cobwebs will be spotted, but that does not mean the world needs to stop.

The children were right: Nobody act small.

Not just children are hungry for medium-acting association; we all are. The world is hungry for people of integrity—whose normalcy is honesty, whose repute is of respect, and whose manner is bold by its simplicity.

We need people of morality—whose demonstrativeness is not known by its negative puritanism but by their "yes" being "yes" and their "no" being "no." We need authentic people whose place in life—whether of high estate or of meager assignment—is pursued with devotion.

There is an old story about a lovely villa on the shore of beautiful Lake Como in the Italian Alps. Some tourists there complimented the trusted old gardener who had maintained the grounds for years. One said, "The owner must come here frequently"—to which the gardener replied, "No, he has been here only once in fifteen years, and then I did not see him."

"But how do you get your orders?" the tourist asked. "From the owner's agent who lives in Milan," the gardener replied.

"Then he must come here often?" said the tourist. "No, perhaps once a year or so," replied the gardener.

The tourist was amazed, responding, "You have no one to supervise your work, and the grounds are as neat as if you expected the owner to come back tomorrow!"

"Today, sir!" the gardener responded firmly. "Not tomorrow, but today."

The gardener was faithful to his trust—acting medium.

Here are some suggestions for how we might act medium: Let us strengthen our connection with Jesus Christ. Thomas Carlyle quoted his father, saying, "What this parish needs is a man who knows Christ other than at secondhand." Jesus, who came into the medium terrain of life to reveal the love of God, gives dignity to the place and station of all who follow him.

Let us strengthen our connection to the body of Christ (the church). Within the body of Christ, each of us is connected to one another (vv. 9–13). As we resolutely function in the task that is uniquely ours to do, and as others do likewise in their tasks, however prominent or however humble it may be, the desire to connect in devotion and loyalty strengthens each of us individually and the church corporately.

Let us strengthen our connection to a broken and needy world. Because of the body of Christ, each of us is connected to the world around us (vv. 14-21).

These are good ways to act medium.

7/28/96

Religion Is a Verb

Deuteronomy 30:15-20; 1 John 4:21

When he came into his ministry, Jesus found a people who were seriously religious. However, being totally devoted to the laws of God, they had become blinded to the God of the laws.

In striving for a level of righteousness, they became proud of their own self-righteousness and their condemning of others who were not as they were. These really religious people exercised a passive greed that issued religion as a closed shop—operative and functional only by a passive elitism.

Within the religious leadership, nepotism was a clergy practice—as was constant surveillance of prophetic and questioning voices. Any questioning of the establishment was thwarted. Temple expulsion of contrary voices was acceptable. Dissenters were, on occasion, crucified. The witness and the influence of religion contradicted the witness and the influence of God.

Unlike God, the representation of these devotees became uncaring of others, condescending in their advocacy, and demeaning to those of lesser light. They went to extreme measures to be "good" (truly religious) to the detriment and exhaustion of their own spirituality. Jesus never had a chance in such a climate.

Their circle was so tight, and their function was so orchestrated. Their mannerism was so calculated that they were untouched by Jesus' glory because their vision was circumscribed by their own self-righteousness.

There was another side to the world of Jesus, however. While the religiously good people turned their backs to Jesus, sinners and outcasts came to him face-to-face. The sinners and outcasts had been told by the religious elite that there was no room for them. The religious people, who supposedly could have seen the glory of God in the person of Jesus, saw not. But blind people saw him.

Those who could hear, heard not. But deaf people heard his every word. Those who could have reached out and touched him treated him as a leper, while lepers were being cleansed by his touch. Thus, Jesus stepped into the breach that had been established between God and the "good" people and between God and the "bad" people.

In relating to the good people, Jesus conveyed to them that there is nothing they could *not* do to make themselves acceptable before God. These good people expected to be judged on two standards. If they could keep the law and the regulations thereof, they felt completely safe. Also, since they were of a certain racial group, they thought they'd be judged with unique favor apart from other races.

To them, Jesus said that the basic conveyance of the law actually reveals that they are sinful, in spite of themselves. Jesus told some good news to the good people: Such striving to keep the law is not necessary.

To these good people, Jesus said: "Relax; you're trying too hard! You are so caught up in your righteousness that you are overplaying your religiosity. Stop foaming at the mouth, rolling in the aisles, stomping your feet, and pounding your breasts. Put an end to your pious strutting as well as your condescending leers."

He told them: "I know I have upset you. On the Sabbath when I healed the man with the withered hand, you thought, 'It shouldn't have been done on the Sabbath.' But when I saw the man, something within me said, 'It must be done.' When I forgave the adulteress and you turned away from stoning her, you shouted, 'But she's a sinner!' Yet I saw the fear upon her face, and I cared for her, and look at her now! Remember Zacchaeus? You said he was a sinner, so you turned the other way in his presence, but I cared for him, and now he cares for you."

Because Jesus cared, he presented a new portrait of God. And the way to God is not in listing the things you do not do. There is no way to lift oneself in God's sight. God doesn't want to hear: "Look, God! See what I don't do? God, see how good I am? I don't do anything!" To the religious Jesus said, "Back off; take a break; come to me!"

In relating to the bad people, Jesus encouraged them to "rev up." Their self-image was low. They had been so despised and denied that they had come to despise and deny themselves. They sensed no hope, felt little honor, and knew no heritage.

So Jesus said to them: "Get with it. You're so caught up in your unrighteousness that you're missing the opportunity for potential goodness. Stop beating your heads against a wall. Straighten up, and fly right. Lift your stooped shoulders. Get with it!"

Jesus added, "I know I have given you hope—because the blind see, the deaf hear, and the leper is clean." Jesus presented a new portrait of God. God is known by what Jesus did.

To the good people Jesus conveyed: "You have no joy in the way you seek to do good; be of good cheer, for I have overcome those forces that goad and despise and abuse you. Remove the false pride, which is so superficial, and come to know the joy of a humble and contrite heart."

To the bad people he conveyed, "Remove your rebellious spirit that is so ridiculous, and know the joy of a glad and wholesome spirit."

Sometimes God gets a bad name by the manners of "good" people. But because Jesus cared, some good people caught on, and their lives were transformed.

Because Jesus cared, some "bad" people caught on. Is it not clear that true religion is a verb? Do we not prove what we say with our lips by what we do with our hands?

11/26/95

The Talent(s) Tally

Matthew 25:14-30

Ben Hogan's success at golf was no accident. Seated next to broadcaster Bud Wilkinson decades ago at a banquet, Wilkinson noticed Hogan shifting his table knife in his hands with various grips. Later, he questioned Hogan about his seemingly nervous antics with the knife.

Hogan said: "During the program, in my mind, I was playing tomorrow's first round in the tournament. By the time I go to bed tonight, I will have played the course thirty times in my head. It was not so much nerves you saw at the table; I was gripping the necessary club for what was going on in my head."

No one will ever question Hogan's legendary talent as a golfer. Though his abilities are remarkable, his championship years were also a testimony to tough mental preparation.

Each of us is created equal in the sense that God intends for all of us to have the chance to attest ourselves. The sacredness of this reality is ensured within our civil and legal rights. Otherwise, each of us is created unequal. Our native, innate, natural abilities are dissimilar. One is a Shakespeare while another is a hack writer. One is a superstar while another is a sandlot bench warmer.

Each of us is unequal in opportunity. Educational options abound for some, while others never move into elementary literacy. Each of us is unequal in advantage, with one the heir of wealth and another with the handicap of poverty.

So we are led to see a self-evident paradox: we are all equal while being unequal. At first glance this seems such a disparity, forever affecting the advantage for the "haves" over the plight of the "have-nots."

However, in the economy of God, a person with one talent, faithfully applied, may reap a harvest beyond a counterpart with five talents. There is indeed a difference in the parable between five and two and one. However, what the landlord commended upon his return was the individual faithfulness with which two servants had functioned.

Each heard, "Well done, good and faithful servant; you have been trustworthy over a few things so I will put you in charge of many things; enter into the joy of your master" (vv. 21, 23).

God does not grade on a curve or by some arbitrary standard. It is not "me against the world" in God's math but rather "me with my ability (talent) against myself, unto the world."

Reflected in the parable is the hard reality that the landlord returns and each account is judged separately, in and of itself. Judgment is an area of life that many today take lightly. Therefore, we hear, "I'm not accountable for abusing my nephew, I was abused as a boy by my uncle"; "I'm not responsible in any way for my lung cancer. Oh, I smoked for forty years, but it is the tobacco industry's doings"; "I'm not to be expected to tithe my income; I don't have the resources of Mr. Got-It-All."

Often we run around our own accountability by blaming others, at times even God. Yet judgment is as much a part of life as the actions we take that lead to its visit. To have been abused does not become a license to abuse. To have willingly dissipated with tobacco, alcohol, drugs, or careless eating habits cannot be someone else's accountability.

To avoid tithing by belittling what we have against what others have makes no biblical or moral sense. What belongs to God that we keep in our own possession, we may think we can use or invest to be a blessing unto us. However, no scheme we devise nor lottery we may win can outperform a promise to our benefit from God.

Listen to God's promise to tithers: "Thus put me to the test, says the LORD of hosts; see if I will not open the windows of heaven for you and pour down for you an overflowing blessing" (Mal. 3:10).

Today's Scripture lesson says much. Especially, it says whatever we are given, we are responsible for it. We are given voices and feet and talents. We share in having been given the single most treasured talent available. We have been given the name of Christ.

Whatever we say to the world around us should echo the voice of Christ. Whatever we do in the world around us should pantomime the hands of Christ. Wherever we go in the world around us should mirror the presence of Christ.

As Christ to the world around us, we await Christ himself—who will judge whether or not we are who we claim to be. What we have been given is serious business—for "to whom much is given, much will be required" (Luke 12:48a). Then Jesus added, "And from the one to whom much has been entrusted, even more will be demanded" (Luke 12:48b).

Another thing is said in today's scripture: Whatever we are given is not for us to hoard, hide, or flaunt. Some of us delight in downplaying ourselves when it comes to the use of our talents. We tend to be more open in the marketplace, often taking risks and extending ourselves to our limits. However, with the things of faith, we often downplay ourselves.

If our income is limited in comparison to the cost of living, we downplay ourselves by saying that "my little" is so little that it doesn't matter whether I give it or not. If our income is significant, we downplay ourselves by saying that "my much" is so in demand that I have to limit my giving.

Chuck Yeager, the famous pilot who first broke the sound barrier, revealed some interesting tidbits from aviation history in his autobiography. One of the most unusual happened at Edwards Air Force Base in the late 1950s. A test pilot, diving in a Mach 2 fighter, actually outraced the shells from his cannons and shot himself down.

That is unusual in an airplane. However, we do it all the time in our lives. Instead of patiently waiting on the Lord, we rush ahead too quickly and end up shooting ourselves down.

In today's Bible lesson the man who was given the one talent chose to bury it. Yet by burying it, he buried himself. By the improper use of our talents, we lose them, thus losing the advantage of experiencing the outpouring of God's blessings upon us.

11/23/97

We Have Good News To Share

Matthew 5:16

How seriously do we consider our charge to be witnesses for Jesus? In light of this passage, and others just as demanding, how do we defend our reticence to give personal, verbal testimony?

By and large, being nonverbal witnesses is not because we are ashamed of our gospel (our good news). After all, in many ways we boldly give testimony as witnesses: We have publicly united with the church. We give our tithes and offerings. We serve as deacons, teachers, and committee members. We visit hospitals. We bring sacks of food for the needy.

Inside this building, and one-on-one with one another, we are steadfast, abounding, verbal—even outspoken—as witnesses for Christ. Yet many of us who are so bold within these walls are tongue-tied and evasive in the marketplace, at the bridge table, on a date, or in a "bull session." Why?

As we approach a season that bears the title Thanksgiving, we will generally feel unencumbered in stating words of thanks in regard to what we call our "blessings." On the other hand, we will allow many seasons of opportunity to pass by without affirming a personal testimony of what God's love can mean in the life of someone who has a need to know what we know.

The first command in the Sermon on the Mount is that we should let our light shine, giving witness to the experiences of the heavenly Father within us. Interestingly, we can be most vociferous and bold in the political arena (knocking on doors for permission to display "our" candidate's name) and in community affairs (making appeals for the United Way, the YMCA, the Chamber of Commerce), yet never feel comfortable in a direct, open affirmation of the most significant commitment we will have ever made in our lives.

Why? Is it that we want to avoid appearing pious? Is it that we fear our testimony may return later to haunt us? I think many of us actually fear being accused of being sanctimonious more than we do of being a rascal.

Augustine, in his "Confessions," admitted that at times he was "ashamed to be blameless." Today, it is popular to be a church attender. Yet an outspoken, energetic avowal of one's faith is viewed suspiciously.

Most of us prefer a witness lifestyle of being laid back, cautious, unambitious. We will energize many of the commands of Jesus, but feel ill equipped to be a spokesman upon his behalf.

In the charge to witness, often we are observers rather than participants. We prefer being in the audience to being on stage. We would rather be present to hear than to be heard. We assume others to be better equipped to be witnesses than we are.

In certain situations or on certain occasions with certain people, however, no one else in the whole wide world could be the witness necessary. There are times when we are "it."

We tend to be clever in rationalizing this charge. We will emphasize our deeds and minimize our words. On the surface this appears to be an act of humility. But who among us lives so purely that our example alone is sufficient as a witness?

Jesus not only charges us to be witnesses, but is the example of our witness. His disciples were to go on a witness trip, and they expressed the concern of not knowing what to do or say. Jesus' response was that they—by their goings and sayings—would be led in their deeds and in their words.

Jesus, we are told, "went about doing good." But he also was constant in verbal witness to individuals, to small groups, and to multitudes. If Jesus, whose life was perfect, gave public, verbal witness, so very much more must we.

Our charge is not to shine that we may be seen. Our charge is to shine so that the Father might be seen in us. Our charge is to get out of the audience and onto the witness stand.

A nineteenth-century industrial baron once said to Mark Twain, "Before I die I mean to make a pilgrimage to the Holy Land. I will climb to the top of Mount Sinai and read the Ten Commandments aloud." Twain, whose bite was deep and whose wit was demanding, said, "I have a better idea: why don't you stay home in New York and keep them?"

Well, how do we go about doing this? We do so in our conversations—forthright, precise, making our words accountable, returnable. We do so in our spirit—one of gentility, light, joy, and peace. We do so in our community—where we pay our debts, mark our ballots, collect our trash, honor our neighbors, tend to our parents, and instruct our children.

Our charge is to be the light in the midst of darkness. Our charge is to make contemporary the love of Christ. And our charge is to speak his name—in the checkout line, on the golf course, at the coffee shop, and across the back fence.

11/21/93

The Bible: God's Story

2 Timothy 3:16-17; 2 Peter 2:20-21

Year by year the Bible remains the best-selling book. No doubt every home represented this morning possesses not just a Bible but one for each person in the family—with most of us owning a number of translations. How the pages of this book are attended is as varied as the interests, intents, and devotion of those of us who possess this precious treasure.

Certain bestsellers and recognized classics are so rich in life associations that we read them almost without putting them down. When new books by certain writers are published, we immediately purchase them because the authors have become heroes or heroines of our literary adoration and appetite. Yet, in time, bestsellers and our heroic editions find places on bookshelves or in closets to collect the dust of time, only rarely retrieved for reference or to sate our nostalgia.

However, the Bible remains readily accessible at arm's reach whether for serious study or a moment of devotion or an occasion of inspiration or a needed reminder of courage, patience, or peace. As the hymn writer John Burton penned of the Bible, "Mine to comfort in distress, Suffering in this wilderness; Mine to show by living faith, We can triumph over death."

As a pastor to people in times of sickness or on the occasions of death in the family, it is the Bible to which we turn or to those epic poems in which people of sensitive faith have left their biblically inspired lines. One of my most difficult occasions is standing adjacent to a casket, seeking to give comfort and hope. But over and over again, I have seen the amazing transformation emerge within a family and among friends when I read from the Bible. I see sorrowing and despairing hearts permeated with comfort.

The Bible has not had an unimpeded, protected journey from the time of its canonization. It is a book that has been burned, banned, and boondoggled. In the fourth century, Diocletian, with the power of the Roman Empire, tried to put the Bible in its grave. Viciously, he killed Christians while burning the literature of their faith.

Thinking the battle had been won, he had a column of triumph erected and inscribed with the following claim: "The name of the Christians has been extinguished." Yet less than twenty years later Diocletian was dead, and the new emperor, Constantine, avowed the Christian faith.

The Bible has been endowed with resistance to withstand damnations of atheists, exaggerations of fanatics, misuses of preachers, unfamiliarity of laity, and discredits of secularists. The more sophisticated the science of archaeology has become, the more reliability has been given to the Bible's testimony to time, geography, and history.

The Bible is an old book. However, in our world its ancient voice has a modern echo. It is no ordinary book. It is the Word of God.

As Karl Barth suggested, today's Christian should hold the daily newspaper in one hand and the Bible in the other hand. As such it is as relevant for the twentieth century as it was in the days it was written.

Do you have any idea the number of times you have read or recited the Twenty-third Psalm? This book is so rich and inexhaustible. Yet not everyone is so awed by it. Many find the Bible to be rather boring, difficult to follow, its settings too foreign, its demands too exacting, its promises too sketchy, and its guidelines too restrictive.

But when we delve seriously into these pages, listen intently to its lessons, and grasp strongly its challenges, we find a richness of spiritual food. No other book can be so deeply mined and continue to produce priceless gems of spiritual nurture.

Therefore, should we worship this resilient, reliant, relevant, rich source of God's Word? No! But indeed we treasure the Bible. It is a vehicle that spans twenty centuries. It is big! We are confronted within its pages by an ongoing story—at times frightening, heroic, deceitful, demeaning, face-saving, guilt-laden, jealous, and courageous.

It is filled with agony, tragedy, defeat, and triumph. As we get caught up in this story, we look in the mirror of our own stories and find that these pages are our pages. Though separated by centuries, our stories are this story. The God who acted among them is acting in our midst.

The Bible is the *Word* of God. More so, the Bible is the *acts* of God together with the human response (reaction) thereto. The Bible, in the course of a lifetime, becomes for many an answer book. However, the Bible also remains forever a question book.

Within this book the star attraction is Jesus Christ. He emerges as the greatest show of God's hand, God's triumphant act. But even Jesus remains a question unless we allow him to answer for us the great questions that only faith can enliven.

It is when we read the Bible and heed its story and find our place in God's loving act of giving his Son as our savior—believing that he acts for us in eternal ways that we cannot act for ourselves—that this big book truly serves its purpose. Indeed, we greatly respect the Bible because of what it points toward. It is the flashlight out of darkness. It is the shoehorn into sandals of faith. It is the avenue routing us from despair to hope. It is the artery flowing us into the river of God. It is the track upon which we join those already running with faith.

The Bible is God's story, a story of God's actions upon our behalf. It is a lamp to our feet and a light to our path—leading us to worship at the altar of God.

2/12/95

Overcoming Our Timidity

Matthew 25:14-30

1 Peter 4:10: "Like good stewards of the manifold grace of God, serve one another with whatever gift each of you has received."

1 Corinthians 12:7: "To each is given the manifestation of the Spirit for the common good."

Ephesians 4:7: "But each of us was given grace according to the measure of Christ's gift."

It is routine for us to excuse ourselves from significant endeavors in the church, and in life itself, by declaring that our gifts are too modest to be significant. When we make such a protest, today's Scripture text from Matthew's Gospel (as well as these words from the Epistles) should ring in our ears.

My first full-time pastorate was in the small village of Alpine, Alabama, in Talladega County. Upon arrival, I met with the deacons (five men). I soon began to sense the lay of the land. Each deacon let me know he could not pray in public.

When I asked who could, with one voice they acclaimed, "Mrs. Mitchell can!" So Mrs. Mitchell and I did all the public praying.

On Sunday evenings I began to meet with the youth on a regular basis. Rather carefully, I called upon them to pray as we began our sessions and as we closed. In time this became an expected and accepted procedure.

Later during worship one Sunday evening, I called on thirteen-year-old Ben Vincent to pray the offertory prayer. He did so in a mumbling yet acceptable manner. The next weekend was my time to spend the night at the Vincent farm. Following the Saturday evening meal Ben's dad, "Red," who was a deacon, invited me to walk with him to the barn.

Walking back to the house, Red said, "Thank you, Jon, for helping my son, at his early age, to express the gift of prayer."

How many gifts are waiting within us that have not been opened because we were not encouraged or called upon—or were left unopened because of a timidity out of fear or the embarrassment of potential failure? The timid soul in today's Scripture lesson had received the least gift in value, perhaps indicating limited expectation. It is evident that he lacked self-confidence.

Having received—let's say—$100,000, he never moved from the notion that it was his master's money, a master who was a hard man and who insisted on a good return from each investment. This fear raised its voice: Suppose he invested in a project that failed or placed the money in a bank that collapsed? Suppose when his boss returned, he could give him only $70,000 in return for what had been entrusted to him?

Timidity distorted his thinking. He feared the reaction of his hard master without thinking that his master had shown confidence in his potential by entrusting him with so great a gift. If his boss had told him what to do, he would have followed the directions to the letter and managed each detail with exacting precision.

But, no, the master gave him the gift with no design attached, simply saying, "Take care of this!" So he did the safe thing: he buried the money in the ground. In a way he was proud of what he had done. He anticipated the return of his master and being able to say, "Here it *all* is, sir, every cent of it, just like you entrusted it to me. Not a penny has been lost."

We're not talking about a bad man here. However, his master ate him alive when he did return, calling him a wicked, lazy servant. You know I'm a tough operator, the master told him. Why didn't you act accordingly?

There is no humor in this story. Jesus is telling us what real life is like. In this parable the loving teacher is the no-nonsense, pragmatic rabbi who talks with us not on the basis of how we wish things were but on the basis of how things are. Jesus is telling us that what we don't use, we lose. It is a simple story of how life works.

Why so timid? What made him like this? Did he come from a long line of defeated people?

In our own society there are pockets of people where defeat is the order of life. No one expects to succeed, and no one expects anyone else to succeed. Was he that kind of person? Did he never have a teacher who inspired him—or a neighbor with a helping hand? Was there no one to encourage him to look up rather than down?

His problem was not that he received only the one talent; his problem was that he didn't use what was given to him. The villain in this parable is not a bad man, but he is a wasteful man. Anyone who wastes life is a villain. Some waste it in obvious ways like the prodigal in a far country. Most of us waste it in socially acceptable ways, which brings us no seeming reproach.

However, Jesus is saying, "Take your thumb out of your mouth! Do something! Use, in the ways only you can, what the King has entrusted to you."

This man we identified as timid is called "lazy and wicked" by his master. For all practical purpose, he is a sinner. We are inclined to define sin in the classic trinity of "thought, word, and deed." But perhaps the most insidious sin, most to be feared, the one so easy to beset us, is our failure to trust God.

In this parable the landowner believed in his servants enough to trust them with various, yet distinct gifts. But the timid soul did not believe in himself, nor did he believe in the landowner's opinion of him.

The angelic chorus in Henrik Ibsen's play *Peer Gynt* chanted to him about a coming judgment: "We are deeds you have left undone, strangled by doubt. Spoiled ere begun. At the Judgment day we shall be there to tell our tale; How will you fare?"

The Master of us all has invested in each of us various and distinctive talents and gifts to be used, expended in his vineyard. How will *we* fare?

2/25/96

God's Call

Genesis 12:1-4a

From childhood we have been taught Abraham's story, that remarkable man of faith who in response to God's call, according to E. M. Blaiklock, "stepped out, abandoned much, found much more and built that nation which, under God, was the people of God's choice; through whom the Bible came, through whom Christ was born, through whom we have been saved."

Joe Callaway, in his book *Faces of the Old Testament* (Smyth & Helwys, 1995), spoke of Abraham meeting "the tests of faith that came in the context of his world and passed them."

We tell and repeat Abraham's ancient story of his call and response and find that his journey, though old, teems with the echoes of our call and response. For him, as for us, it was and is a paradoxical trek: at times clear, at other times confusing; at times with hope, at other times in despair; at times real, at other times uncertain; at times victorious, at other times a failure.

Abraham struggled with his call, asking, "Why me, Lord?" He had to be constantly prodded by the Lord: "Yes, you Abraham. It is I who called you!"

The call of God is not coercive. God's call leaves room for refusal, for implicit obedience, or for obedience with reservation. However, if God's call is followed, there is an expectation of utter and unquestioned obedience.

Abraham chose, initially, to respond to God's call with obedient reservation. Let me pause to make this observation: Abraham was a layman. He was not being called into professional ministry. He was called to follow God's directive in the basic vocation of his being. He was farmer, herdsman—responsible as a patriarch for himself and for his family's well-being, through which he opened himself up to God's leadership.

Let us hold on to what Abraham was (a farmer, herdsman) and what he did (lived an authentic life). The relevance of his status is not that he lived an ascetic life, sealed off from harsh realities, but that he went forth—not knowing where he was going—because he believed in the one who bid him to go.

His life was authentic; he drank of the life that he encountered in his world and passed the tests of faith that we meet in our own circumstances. To respond to God's call is costly. Abraham was compelled to leave his home and take only moveable possessions. He said goodbye to relatives and friends while surrendering his social and communal status—doing so at an advanced age.

This raises the question of God's call and our age. Are we ever too old or too young to hear God's call? Abraham was old; Jeremiah claimed God called him while in his mother's womb. Between the womb and the tomb, God calls.

Whatever one may be compelled to give up, however, the response to God's call opens doors to possibilities that otherwise would have been unavailable. More likely than not, the blessings accrued will not be solely for the faithful respondent. From faithful Abraham came forth the nation Israel, the incarnation of God's Son, the church, our being present in this place, this hour. A tiny pebble, tossed into a lake, sends ripples to the total circumference of the shorelines. No call of God is of little consequence.

Jesus said those of us who feed "the least of these" feed him. I dare say all of us have responded to the call of Christ to feed the hungry. And when, in faith, we have been compelled to do so, we have no way of knowing the ripple effect.

We should judge less and condemn not the hungry and homeless. It is easy enough to indulge our appetites and condemn their appetites. However, with a full stomach and with God's Spirit, our loaf of bread could be that pebble cast upon the pond of existence, engendering hope and self-worth.

Abraham's faithful response to God's call became a model for the founding and the establishment of a nation of people that became the people of God. From the womb of that nation, patriarchs came forth affirming allegiance to the God of Abraham; judges came forth prescribing laws worthy of tribute to the God of Abraham; kings came forth who ruled in favor of the God of Abraham; prophets came forth who compelled the straying people of God to return to the God of Abraham; a savior came forth born into the lineage of David, possessing the seed of Abraham; and the church came forth as the remnant of God's people with an urge to spread to all people the saving power of the God of Abraham.

In 1830 fifteen people founded this church as one of the manifold seeds of Abraham, celebrative of the faith of Abraham who left Ur of the Chaldees some 2,945 years ago in obedience to the call of God.

Earlier, we recognized Sunday school teachers and dedicated their endeavor to God, who has called them to teach.

Time, events, circumstances, people, and the prevailing leadership of God will confirm their faith and action. They are as pebbles cast into the pools of our lives, and their witness will ripple to the shorelines of our lives. Thanks be to God!

8/27/95

Sermons from the Gospel of John

"Dr. Appleton was taking summer study at Princeton when he decided that he would like to close his career by preaching through the Gospel of John... He believed it to be a good way to say goodbye."

—Ernest C. Hynds, *Always Becoming New: A History of First Baptist Church, Athens, Georgia* (Nashville: Fields Publishing, 2011) p.346.

Jesus' First Sign

John 2:1-11

Many teachers and advertisement people illustrate their subject matter. The writer of the Gospel of John did the same. Toward the end of his writing, he confessed, "These are written so that you may come to believe that Jesus is the Messiah, the Son of God, and that through believing you may have life in his name" (20:31).

John's message was that Jesus is the Son of God. To prove his point he set forth a number of "signs." Other Gospel writers called them "miracles" or "wonders" or "acts of power." But to this writer they were "signs"—leveling the truth that Jesus was indeed the Son of God.

The first sign was the changing of water into wine at a wedding in Cana of Galilee. It is a simple story, which if read hurriedly might bring an appreciative nod and perhaps a comment such as, "Wasn't that something?" However, we must be careful when reading the Bible, especially passages like this one. We need to pause long enough to become a participant in its drama. It is a sign once given, but it becomes a sign ever alive.

The water was changed into wine at a wedding feast.
Jesus was perfectly at home at a party. He was not a killjoy. He delighted in a good time. Jesus is not portrayed as an anemic ascetic or a prune-faced recluse, withdrawn from the world. Some referred to him as "a glutton and a drunkard, a friend of tax collectors and sinners" (Luke 7:34). Jesus was a happy Savior, a laughing Lord.

When Moses came to Pharaoh, the first sign he did was to turn water into blood (signifying the anger/wrath of God). When Jesus began his ministry, the first sign he did was to turn water into wine (signifying the joy of God).

Jesus was a man of joy. As we participate in this joyous occasion, his first sign, we need to put forth our joyous faces.

This sign happened in a humble cottage in a small village in rural Galilee.
It was not wrought against the backdrop of some great event nor in the presence of vast crowds to impress the noted and the elite. It is disclosed in an ordinary family experiencing a festive circumstance that bordered on disaster.

The sign reveals the hidden glory of Jesus, the Son of God. The recorder of this first sign reveals that water is wine because Word has become flesh; an hour that had not yet come is here.

John knows from the experience of years that to believe in Jesus as the Christ is to live life within life. And Jesus chose to first reveal his inherent glory in inconspicuous surroundings. It was wrought in the setting of a humble home.

A. H. N. Green-Armytage, in his book *A Portrait of St. Luke*, says in a vivid phrase that Luke's Gospel "domesticated" God; it brought God right into the home circle, into the ordinary things of life. When Jesus changed the water into wine, it was the very first time that he "manifested forth his glory." And it took place in an uphill country home.

Home for us is a strange paradox. We agree there is no place like home, sweet home. Songs have been written to express our feelings about home. Yet in that sweet, sweet place, on occasion, some bitter, bitter pills are handed out. It can be a place for discourtesy, for impoliteness, for selfishness, or for boorishness to a degree far beyond how we relate outside the home toward a total stranger.

It was in a home that Jesus manifested forth his glory. For him such a place called forth his best; nothing else was good enough. When Jesus was born, his bed was a stable's manger. Should it surprise us that his first sign was in a humble cottage in a small village in rural Galilee? Jesus chose to go all out in such a place. Why shouldn't we?

Why did Jesus do what he did?

Hospitality in the Middle East was a sacred duty. It would have been a great embarrassment upon that humble household had it been announced that the wine had run out. We need to tread slowly here and get into the rhythm of John's revelation.

Is John revealing to us that in an obscure village, two miles from nowhere, the one who was to be the savior of the world first manifested his glory? John says "yes" to our inquiry.

We prize ourselves in our grand openings and our grand entries as ways to reveal our grand occasions. However, Jesus' grand occasion was without fanfare or bright lights. He chose to reveal his ultimate hand of power simply to save a Galilean boy and girl from humiliation during their wedding festivities.

The changing of water into wine was a big deal. Imagine its grandeur and on such a small scale. Jesus came with so much to give, and, if you heard the story, only the five disciples realized what had happened. The servants just did what they were told to do. The chief steward got so caught up in his first taste that he didn't even ask where it came from. The bridegroom certainly was thinking about other things.

Even Mary, the mother of Jesus, just wanted him to do something in the emergency. But the writer closes by saying, "But his disciples believed in him" (v. 11).

John drops into our minds a remarkable sign, a visual of the extraordinary amid an ordinary emergency. Beneath the sign's subtitles we perceive the length to which God's love will go to provide for our common lives—bringing an uncommon touch and grace and goodness.

When Jesus did what he did, its glory was lost to most everyone present. But it was not lost to his disciples who saw and believed. Today's questions are: Do we see? Do we believe? Only believe!

1/26/97

The Angry Jesus

John 2:13-17

Through the centuries many have argued that Jesus was not truly human. The Gnostics and Docetists gathered great followings from those who could not envision God's Son as being any other than a spiritual, even symbolic presence.

However, John's report of Jesus cleansing the temple—angrily, forcefully, blatantly in the face of acceptable temple practices, while acting as a ruffian—reveals the stark humanity of the man.

Pilgrims came from the known world to Jerusalem. These Jews of devotion—loyal in faith, demonstrative in allegiance, devoted to prescribed law—desired to make sacrifices in the temple. So temple practice offered them a means to that end.

Literally within feet of the altar of sacrifice, what they needed was herded into place and caged within reach: sheep, oxen, and doves. What they purchased had to be bought with temple coins of which none of them possessed. So the temple provided moneychangers who offered the temple coinage in exchange for coinage from around the world.

By temple precedent the availability of animals and the coinage exchange procedure were of benefit to pilgrims and to temple practice alike. Into this arena Jesus came and went berserk! He exclaimed, "Stop making my Father's house a house of trade!"

Why? The altar of sacrifice and worship was nearby, in earshot of animal sounds and smells; of business transactions in the bartering of coinage value; and of selling animals, which by law had to be without blemish—thus evoking close and no doubt, at times, high-voltage argumentation.

Jesus sensed that his Father's house was being desecrated.
He sensed worship without reverence. And without reverence, worship can be a shoddy thing. In the best of circumstances, decor and quietness, the worship of God is a demanding act. Jesus felt the distraction and assailed its source. The temple was not to have been a place of distraction.

Jesus also sensed that his Father's house was being used irrelevantly.
He sensed worship without serviceability. Isaiah had said it eight centuries earlier: "Bring no more vain offerings" (1:7). Hosea had taught, "They love

sacrifice; they sacrifice flesh and eat it, but the LORD has not delight in them" (8:13).

Jesus sensed sacrifice not as a means to the heart of his Father, unless the hearts of those making sacrifice were attuned to God's requirement for those who worship him "to do justice, and to love kindness, and to walk humbly with your God" (Mic. 6:8).

Jesus also sensed that his Father's house was being used primarily as a marketplace.
He sensed worship without inclusiveness. In Mark's Gospel Jesus is reported to have said, "My house shall be called the house of prayer for all nations" (11:17).

There was one and only one place non-Jews could attend the temple: the Court of the Gentiles. And in that court, within the confines of the temple but at its outer perimeter, is precisely where the temple business was stationed.

If all nations are to be included within the house of prayer, then seeking people of all races were being rudely excluded from their prescribed place by the lack of reverence and the irrelevant clutter that blocked them from their search.

Jesus' hot anger, his show of force, and his incautious command to "Stop!" were avowed rejections of the temple system as too much of a marketplace. God's favor, nor protection, can be purchased with sacrifices or sanctioned by priestly hierarchy.

The angry Jesus in this context, and on other occasions in the Gospels, comes through when religion becomes irrelevant or when people are exploited. Jesus is never angry out of his own self-centeredness or for his own personal desires.

We must allow the angry Jesus to inspire our anger. Bede Jarrett wrote: "The world needs anger. The world often allows evil to continue because it isn't angry enough."

In our own house of worship, we gather not to be so formal that we perish the thought for change. We pray not words as though reading a passage from an auctioneer's catalogue. We worship in God's holiness—never casually, as though we think of God as our pal.

There are occasions for us to be contentious about those things that are besetting—but never to be argumentative as within the marketplace nor to be so callous as to contend for our ways regardless.

In our own house of worship, we must be conscious of our gifts given, not as means to acquire God's favor nor to impress one another. Our gifts are love offerings from the heart, symbols of our devotion.

In our own house of worship, we are to do all things possible to be inclusive. Seekers are to find us with opened arms, welcomed by words and helping hands.

In our own house of worship, these and other Christian virtues are to be lived. And if not, we should be enjoined by the angry Jesus.

2/2/97

The Father and the Son

John 5:19-20, 30

It is difficult to overstate how awesome are these words of our Lord found in John's Gospel. George Buttrick called them "the tremendous claims of Jesus."

Because we live this side of the resurrection and are privy to the whole gospel, we know the truth of these claims. In no way did Jesus overstate his relation to the Father.

Imagine, however, taking your place on that Sabbath there in the streets of Jerusalem. How staggering his claims, how audacious his confession! Listen to an overview of Jesus' claims: an absolute unity of mind and will with God—and an emphatic declaration that to reject Jesus is to turn one's back on God.

There is a calm assertion that it is God's will "that all may honor the Son, even as they honor the Father." These claims do not stagger us, though they should. Had we been present along with the religious authorities who questioned him that day, we would have been astounded by such claims.

One piece of evidence might have cautioned our denial of his claims, had we the insight to perceive such presence. While none of us is now astounded when reading or hearing these claims, we ought to pray for a sense of awe. If so, these words could in some way continually create wonder and the reeling of our minds and the provocation of our wills.

We would be more alive to the Son and to the Father in times both ordinary and extraordinary—in days of common and uncommon living. We who affirm these claims of Jesus believe his pronouncements to be true. However, often we avail not ourselves of the mighty power his confession puts within our reach.

The Son brings the Father into our company here, where we live. Jesus knows the mind of the Father and would willingly make that mind known unto us. Jesus knows the will of the Father and would willingly make that will known unto us.

Let me address here what came to my mind as I was preparing today's message: There are indeed times, many, many times, when we do call upon the Son and the Father—pleading for their mind and their will to be made plain to us.

We do believe that God the Father and God the Son are uniquely blended to be on call for us in our times of difficulty, distress, and despair. Yet when we are having a good day, let us seek the mind of the Son and the Father to make the good day a better one.

When we have been especially blessed, let us seek the mind of the Son and the Father to convey our blessing to someone who would benefit from our sharing. When we are having a good thought, let us connect our mind to the Son and the Father to build upon it for a grander, perhaps deeper thought.

When we amid life's struggles have found peace, let us seek the mind of the Son and the Father to deepen that grace so we may continue to be nurtured. When we are having a good day, let us enjoin the will of the Son and the Father so that goodness may be extended for a season.

Having been blessed by the joy of fellowship, may we be led of will to share the joy with those who abide in distress. Having been blessed by an act of kindness, may we be led of will to share kindness with those who are strangers to kindness.

Having been boosted by an act of generosity, may we be led of will to share a boost to another who is in need. Having been cautioned to desist from sin, may we be led of will to share our fortune of caution with someone who is living recklessly.

Most everyone listening to my voice could stand at this moment and bear witness to the Son's and the Father's benevolent response amid times of anxiety, illness, and distress. My concern, for myself and for everyone, is that with the Son and the Father so availing to us in our distresses and weaknesses, why do we not invoke their company amid our victories and good fortune?

Being witnesses to God's prevailing grace in our times of woes, do we not see our good fortune to be in the Son's and the Father's company when the wind at our back is good, when the harvest is abundant, when the market rebounds, when our children find happiness, when our health is vibrant, and when our vision is focused?

I believe that should we call upon the Son and the Father day in, day out; in sunshine, in rain; in plenty, in need; in victory, in defeat; in joy, in sorrow—then the blessings of heaven would pour down upon us.

May we not grow weary in our days of distress nor complacent in our days of blessing. Nothing would be weighed upon us that could not be lifted; no bounty could be our fortune that would engender within us a selfish or a mean spirit. No disadvantage would limit us nor any advantage distract us from the grace of the Son and the Father, who are with us through darksome valleys and beside us on victorious mountaintops.

Jesus' "tremendous claims" found in today's Scripture lesson bring into our lives his deeds that are reenactments of the things God goes about doing. Jesus relates that those things God is doing and the things that he, himself, does emanate from love. And as grand as those things the Father and the Son have done, even greater things will be shown.

How could we neglect so grand a witness by our belief, our obedience, our quest? Call upon the name of the Lord who is near; call out to the Son who will reveal to us the Father.

11/2/97

Mercy

John 8:1-11

One morning a number of religious leaders in Jerusalem had gathered at the house of one of them—for what in modern understanding and language would be to come up with a way to take care of a serious problem. The issue was Jesus of Nazareth, and those gathered were the leadership elite who had the clout and had assumed the responsibility of coming to an agreement on how to deal with such an irregular but popular teacher.

Jesus, on more than one occasion, had defied their authority, had responded to them rudely, and had spoken as though his teachings could add to their holy, sacred, and inerrant tradition. While debating their options, they heard a disturbance outside, followed by rapid knocks at the door. In came officials, dragging with them a woman screaming and clawing hysterically.

When order was somewhat restored, the intruders were asked to explain this unusual interruption. Pointing to the woman one said, "This hussy was just caught in the very act of adultery. In olden days we could have rightfully stoned her. But now the Roman governor will not let us. Only you, gentlemen, can tell us what to do with her."

It was suggested that she be removed from the house along with those who had brought her so the recognized ones in authority could resolve so serious an issue. As quietness was restored, one spoke with a sparkle in his eyes, saying, "What a Godsend!" All eyes turned to the spoken voice, addled by his unusual pronouncement and widening smile.

He who spoke, time after time, had arisen to bring them together when insight was needed and wisdom mattered. So he spoke again: "Come, come fellows. Don't you see? Our prayers are answered. The reason for gathering this morning was to gain a consensus in dealing with this Jesus of Nazareth. This woman has been dropped into our laps. Let's go to the temple where he is teaching. We'll take her, state her offense, and call upon him to determine her fate. Should he side with mercy, we have him. Should he avow her being stoned, the Romans have him. Either way, he will be yesterday's news by tomorrow."

How interesting the energy expended by those who would perpetuate place, position, and power. How quickly minds can turn to translate the sin of one, not only to snare the guilty party but to indict someone else who is innocent within the context of the other's guilt. The woman became for them a tool to get at Jesus, who had so elusively avoided their snare.

How frightened are people who maintain their position and power by contriving means to belittle and entrap others.

Public hangings do not crime deter nor righteousness engender. Leaving a policeman dead or a nurse deformed at an abortion clinic is ridicule for the Right to Life issue. Saying that AIDS is God's judgment on homosexuality is an affront to God and an indignity not just to homosexuals but to the entire human race. Claiming master status for the male in marriage is the voice of frightened men in a troubled society and of befuddled women in a convoluted gender bias that makes an enigma of Holy Scripture.

Scripture is used to validate human institutions, human bias, and human mores contrary to the spirit of the Lord. Frightening is the potential for using Holy Writ as a tool to maintain position and power or to maim unduly the guilty or to falsely accuse the innocent.

When the religious leaders left that house with the woman in tow to confront Jesus at the temple, they climbed the hill with Scripture on their side, or so it seemed to them. Indeed, they presented their case against her and requested of Jesus his verdict. What did Jesus say about the woman?

He made no reply. He kept silence. Jesus looked neither at the accusers nor at the accused. Rather, "he bent down and wrote with his finger on the ground."

What did he write? The laws of Moses? Laws applicable to those who had been violated by the accusers as well as by the one accused?

Frederick Neumann, a mid-century pulpiteer in Brooklyn, offered an interesting suggestion—that Jesus was doodling! Doodling is an expression of boredom. Jesus would not have anything to do with the fake problem they had brought before him. Not only that, they had done it from ill will against him.

But Jesus was not concerned for himself. Jesus was concerned for the hypocrites themselves and for the people who depended on their teaching. He realized that what they needed most was humiliation. The most abashing treatment for a teacher of the Law was to be confuted in public, so that is what they had to suffer now for their own good.

Jesus said, "Let him who is without sin among you be the first to throw a stone at her." Then cutting off any possible excuse on their part, he bent down again to write with his finger on the ground. All was silent again. And through the silence the words Jesus had spoken sounded and resounded until they pierced the hard shell of the Pharisees' consciences.

One by one they went away, first the elder men and then the younger. What a pathetic procession! They had come as a crowd. They left one by one as the word of Jesus was splitting up the self-righteous crowd into individuals, each one of them ashamed of his own sin. They had come to judge the woman and trap Jesus. They left the woman with Jesus, bearing the burden of their own sinfulness.

For whose benefit has this revelation been made? It is for all who are exposed to sensual temptation. And that includes everyone: "For every one who looks at a woman lustfully has already committed adultery with her in his heart" (Matt. 5:28).

The Law of God must be applied to our own heart first. And the purpose of its heavy sanctions, as instruments of divine revelation, is not the punishment of the law-breaker but rather the creation of character and disposition that makes the breaking of the law inappropriate.

That is what the accredited teachers of the Law had entirely missed—hence their self-righteousness and hypocrisy. Hence their confusion as they were now leaving the scene in bashful silence, one by one. When Jesus looked up, all the accusers had gone. He was left with a bundle of trembling humanity.

"Woman, where are they?" he asked. "Has no one condemned you?" "No one, Lord," she said. "Neither do I condemn you," he said; "go, and do not sin again."

Let us listen carefully to that very brief and weighty pronouncement: "Neither do I condemn you." Her would-be judges had, with the fact of their silent withdrawal, thrown the matter out of court.

Jesus was not an appointed judge. It was not up to him to deal with the legal aspects of the woman's sin. Thus, the literal application of the Law was dismissed not by theory but by the fact that there was nobody left to apply it literally.

Jesus' sole interest was in the person of the woman, the heavenly Father's stray child. What could he do for her? Jesus did not for a moment condone the woman's sin. He did not give her absolution, though his words imply his readiness to give her absolution if she sought it.

What did he do? He applied to the woman the Law of God as he understood it. He taught her what she needed most: penance.

What is the proper penance? In the words of Martin Luther, nailed to the chapel door of Wittenberg Castle at the very beginning of the Reformation, "Not to do it again is the right penance."

Jesus Christ came not to abolish the Law but to fulfill it: "Go, and do not sin again." When he charged the adulterous woman to radically break with her past, to entirely change her way of life for good, what did he do to her? Jesus truly fulfilled the divine commandment that required the execution of adulterers. He who was really without sin was the first to throw at her a stone, the spiritual stone to hit and kill her sin.

To turn away from one's sinful habits gives pain. It means death, more agonizing than physical pain and death. Yet through this pain and death, and through it only, leads the way to life, health, and eternal well-being. If we are prepared to learn judging ourselves by the Law of God, we shall be judged by the same mercy that instead of condemning the adulterous woman threw at her the stone of saving love.

Blessed is the child of God, whatever his or her sin, who suffers the stoning of Jesus. Blessed is everyone whom Christ separates from the crowd of self-righteous sin-baiters to make him a responsible individual who repents of his sins.

Blessed are those who are deadly hit by the word of Christ, for they will live in the power of the word of Christ. May we all let the old man and the old woman in us die and a new life rise through Jesus Christ, our crucified and risen savior.

7/26/98

To See or Not To See

John 9

God did the unheard-of through Jesus, giving sight to a person blind from birth. God can give us what we have never had. The writer of John's Gospel places his whole testimony on such evidence.

Jesus is to be believed in (v. 36) once he has been "seen." So is the testimony of this Gospel (v. 37). The axiom of New Testament faith is "against a fact there is no argument."

For the man who received his sight, Jesus "spat on the ground and made mud with the saliva and spread the mud on the man's eyes, saying to him, 'Go wash in the pool of Siloam.' Then he went and washed and came back able to see" (vv. 6–7).

Do we recognize the marvel of this miracle? Never since the world began has it been heard that anyone opened the eyes of a person born blind. Even in Jesus' day certain eye disorders were curable, but if a person were born blind, it was a permanent condition. This is the underlying point of the story. This man's problem was permanent; he had no hope of ever being able to see; there was no known deliverance.

The relativity of the truth in Scripture, for me, lies in our being able to "see" its stories, lessons, and themes translated into the stories of our own lives or in the lives of others (past and present). As miraculous as this story is, it would only be a myth out of the past unless the themes and lessons of the story can be recognized in subsequent history and in our own existential faith experiences.

That God was in Christ reconciling the world unto himself (2 Cor 5:19) was not confined to a brief three-year tour of Jesus, to register significant moments in his time so we, twenty centuries later, could only look back over our shoulders with awe and in wonder.

As God was in Christ during the ministerial years of Jesus, God continues through the Spirit to be reconciling us. If the reconciling nature of God was limited simply to the earthly sojourn of Jesus, what if any importance would it have for us today?

However, it is important for people today, blinded by circumstances in their lives, to present themselves unto reconciliation. Thereby, they are encountered by one who digs around in the ground, spits on a pile of scooped dust, makes a mud cake, dabs it upon blinded eyes, and sends them to Siloam. And those who have been so treated will return with 20/20 vision.

In Lincoln, Nebraska, in 1991, the grand dragon of the Ku Klux Klan, Larry Trapp, began sending threatening messages to a rabbi, an African-American woman who was publicly known because of her political activism, and an Asian professor at the University of Nebraska. His notes made clear that they were not welcome in Lincoln. He let them know that he knew where each person lived. He was so blinded by hatred that he threatened them and their families if they remained in Lincoln.

The notes were turned over to the police. Aware of Klan activities in that part of the country, they told these persons to take the threats seriously and be cautious about their activities and those of their children. If you had been one of the three, what would you have "seen"—a chance to run, a place to hide, or an opportunity to confront?

The rabbi, Michael Weisser, refused to be intimidated. He began calling the grand dragon's home telephone number. He would have to listen to ten minutes of racist, anti-Semitic venom before he got to the beep, but then he would leave his message. He called again and again.

One day he left a message, saying, "I know who you are and that you're disabled. Don't you realize that the Nazis to whom you pledge allegiance put the disabled on their list of persons who didn't have the right to live?"

Finally, one day the rabbi called, and the man actually answered the phone. They began to talk. During that conversation, Trapp said, "Quit harassing me. I hate you. I don't want anything to do with you."

Weisser responded by saying, "I know that you are disabled. I'm wondering if you have a difficult time getting groceries and taking care of other things that I might be able to help you with."

There was a long silence. The grand dragon wasn't prepared for the rabbi's kindness. He said, "I don't need the help. It's taken care of, but thank you for making the offer."

The rabbi didn't give up. He kept calling and kept talking. Finally, one night the grand dragon called Weisser back and said, "I'd like to get out of the Klan, but I don't know how to do it." The rabbi asked if he'd eaten dinner, and when Trapp said no, Weisser and his wife packed up a meal and went to the man's home.

They took the food in, and that night a strange friendship began forming. Over time, through conversations with the rabbi, the grand dragon began to see how blind he was and how wrong the white supremacists' views were. He told the rabbi stories of how he had been taught hatred as a young child, of things that had happened to him that he had internalized.

He told Weisser how he came to believe that his role in life was to create as much hatred in Lincoln, Nebraska, and that part of the United States as he possibly could. But he now realized how wrong he was, and in a public meeting he denounced the Klan and asked the rabbi, the African-American woman, and the Asian professor if they could possibly forgive him. And they did.

In news articles in 1993, Trapp exposed the goals and methods of the Klan. He said he feared the Klan's plan to not only spread hatred but also their intent to do violent acts of terrorism against blacks and Jews and other groups.

When asked why he reached out to Trapp, Rabbi Weisser responded, "That's what God requires of me. I have to love this man even though I hate his destructive acts."

Jesus said to his disciples, when asked about the cause of the man's blindness, that out of the man's blindness, "God's works can be revealed in him" (v. 3b). We are not to know over the last twenty centuries how many times the biblical story of the blind man has been reenacted as a reconciling episode. It cannot be bound by only the testimony of Christians.

That Rabbi Weisser is Jewish counters not what he did as a gospel story, a reconciling episode. The rabbi's story sounds like a fairy tale, doesn't it? Yes, it does. But it is a true reconciliation tale, by one who knew about being washed at Siloam.

The man born blind was asked by Jesus, "Do you believe in the Son of Man?" Then the man asked of Jesus, "And who is he, sir? Tell me so that I may believe in him."

Jesus then said to him, "You have seen him," and the man answered, "Lord, I believe." And the man then worshiped Jesus.

Please! Please! Whatever burden you bear—your blind spot, family malfunction, loss of a loved one, joblessness, sickness—make yourself available to the touch of Jesus. If you will, there is no telling how you will be reconciled.

Jesus may send you away with mud in your eyes. If so, head straight to Siloam and wash it away. You will not only see, but there is no telling what you might see. The blind man was able to see the source of his salvation.

And there is no telling what you will end up doing. If you have lost something, do not be blinded by your loss. Anger will not restore it; regret will not find it; tears will not restore it; guilt will not reclaim it; running will not bring it back.

Come to the one God has sent—and let him send you to wash away your blindness so that God's works can be revealed in you. Set up an old easel and with old brushes and new paint begin to see again, or sit down with pen in hand and write down those rhymes that have ricocheted in your mind.

Or have the courage to go to an estranged friend and confess, "I may have wronged you, or you may have wronged me, but now it doesn't matter because what I see is tomorrow; yesterday is not even a memory."

Jesus came to offer us precisely this kind of sight. To receive it you only need to wash away the mud. It is up to us to see or not to see.

9/6/98

Unbind Him! Let Him Go!

John 11:38-44

"Loose him! Let him go!" With those words of Jesus, the story of raising Lazarus from the dead concludes.

At one level the story could not end with anything else but such a command, for it recounts that Lazarus came out of the tomb with "his hands and feet bound with linen bandages, his face wrapped in a cloth" (v. 44). For Lazarus to have gone anywhere, someone would have needed to untie the restraints.

At another level, however, it does seem to be something of a downbeat ending. Hearing Jesus' order to loosen Lazarus, one would think that the writer would have shared the crowd's reaction or at least conveyed Lazarus's reunion with his sisters, Mary and Martha. Yet we do not read anything like that. All we have is Jesus' command. Are we then left with just "loose ends"?

Within days after this remarkable miracle, Jesus himself was to experience death and be triumphantly raised from that death. Could there then be something more significant than the simple instruction to the bystanders to release Lazarus from the chords that bound his shroud so he could freely move about?

The clue to this possibility is the word *loose*, which in Greek can be interpreted in one of the following ways: (1) physically untying something; and/or (2) figuratively of being released, including release from sin. For example, Revelation 1:5 reads, "To him who loves us and has set us free from our sins." It appears that this figurative image could indicate that Jesus is not only saying to remove his burial bonds so he can move about freely, but also saying that he is now free from the randomness, the chaos, the distortion, the destructiveness, and the death that sin brings.

If indeed we note this message in the command of Jesus—"Loose him! Let him go!"—then the ending of the story becomes a powerful portrayal of the heart of the gospel. For the gospel story is all about release from sin to freedom and eternal life.

Quickly, we must assert that this does not mean we shall escape death. Ultimately, Lazarus did die again, as will we all. What it does mean is that we shall escape the dower of death; therefore, death need not necessarily hold any fear for us.

In the Episcopal tradition there is a popular canticle titled "Savior of the World." A line in the hymn asserts, "In the greatness of your mercy loose us from our chains; forgive the sins of all your people." This is a most powerful image. What Jesus brings to us is nothing less than a release—a setting free, an unbinding. As we hear these momentous words—"Loose him! Let him go!"—we can pray, "Loose us! Let us go!"

A college student in 1974 told me about the chain that bound her. Years ago a woman in Alabama confessed her bondage to alcohol. A blind man shouted to gain the attention of Jesus, and when Jesus asked him what he could do for him, the man shouted, "I want to see again; loosen the bandages from my blind eyes." The bystanders were commissioned to set Lazarus free.

Days later, when Jesus was crucified and buried, he cried from the cross, "It is finished!" Those gathered around his cross, upon hearing his cry, no doubt thought their own thoughts.

"It is finished!" thought the beloved disciple, "and I loved him so much." "It is finished!" thought his mother, "and I can remember the night he was born."

"It is finished!" Pilate was told, "and I hope I never have to deal with another Messiah." "It is finished!" thought the centurion, "and what a marvelous man he must have been."

"It is finished!" thought the repentant thief hanging beside him, "and I will be with him in paradise." "It is finished!" the Pharisees were told. "That will teach rabble-rousers to mess with us," they shouted.

But when Jesus cried "It is finished!" none was aware that Jesus was acclaiming, "I came down from heaven not to do my own will, but the will of him who sent me" (John 6:38).

Finished were the rages of sin that bind—holding captive all of us until the final assault of death. But the death of Jesus, cruel and undeserving as it was, brought to life God's will to which his Son was totally committed.

Years later, Paul perceived God's plan through these remarkable words: "Where, O death, is your victory? Where, O death, is your sting? The sting of death is sin, and the power of sin is the law. But thanks be unto God, who gives us the victory through our Lord Jesus Christ" (1 Cor. 15:55–57).

The bystanders were charged to set Lazarus free. Someone had to do for him what he could not do for himself.

In the death of Jesus, he loosens us and sets us free. No more do we live under condemnation. He has loosed us and set us free. And the only way we can be bound beyond his love is to refuse to accept his saving death for us.

10/25/98

On Being Extravagant

John 12:1-8

A wife and husband were in a heated argument one morning as he was dressing to leave for work. "When you back your new Porsche out of the garage to go to work, I want you to remember that without my money, you'd still be driving that ole rattletrap you had when we married," she said to him.

Then she added, "And when you play golf this afternoon, I want you to remember that without my money, you'd still be living in a one-bedroom apartment rather than in this palatial palace."

As the husband tugged on his coat to leave, he turned to his wife and said, "There is really only one thing I want you to remember: without your money, I wouldn't be your husband."

Many of us have given ourselves to God in the same spirit of that husband to his wife. We go through the motions of our relationship with God only because we have enough judgment to know that without God's blessings, we would be nothing. We use God only as we need God.

God is our seatbelt for collisions, our parachute for emergencies, our life preserver for choppy waters, our springboard for recognition, our vote of confidence, and our advocate for life. Without what God does for us—offering provisions—we really wouldn't be God's people.

But to use God only when needed is to abuse the generosity of God's benevolence, the grace of God's goodness, and the guarantee of God's salvation.

God is extravagant toward us. But what is our response to God's extravagance? Intuition is an existential experience that is hard to define. It just happens. Something within us, at times, becomes sensitive to a feeling not akin to normal perception. Rather, it is perceived as a voice or an urge within us. We simply know that something is astir and possible—and the awareness defies logic.

Martha responded to an urge to *do* something for Jesus because of what Jesus had done for her family in raising Lazarus from the dead. Her response was partly intuition toward his extravagance. But more so it was an occasion for Martha to be Martha.

Her gifts and talents were practical. The kitchen was her throne from which a kingdom kind of tribute could be served. Her grace was an intuitive response. The celebration, through her practical talents, could be seen and appreciated, heard and rejoiced over, tasted and delighted in. Such a gracious talent is not to be maligned.

Angelic in mission are those who in crises and in victories know how to give a party. Martha's response to the joy in the household was to serve the Master of that joy with food for his body. So the gifted hostess gave a dinner banquet of festive proportion for the honored guest, Jesus, who had by spoken word, as the Bread of Life, called her brother forth from his tomb.

Then there is Mary. Within the family Mary was quite different from Martha. On another occasion (Luke 10) Martha asked Jesus to scold Mary for absenting herself from what, according to Martha, were the necessary chores of the household. But Jesus responded, "Martha, you fret and worry too much, being distracted by many things. Mary will help you, in time, but right now she is grappling with things which are of eternal value."

Could it have been on that occasion that Mary, entranced by listening to Jesus, intuitively, amid the wonder of his words, caught also the pathos of his journey? Perhaps when Jesus spoke of his "glory," it was Mary who understood that he was speaking of his death. When Jesus returned to Bethany, it was Martha who first ran to greet him, and when, at Lazarus' tomb, Jesus commended that the stone be rolled away, it was Martha, not Mary, who pleaded with him not to do so.

Martha, the perfect host, was a greeter of guests and a counselor of caution. But not Mary. Why?

Mary, so attuned to the movement of Jesus, knew why he had returned to Bethany. He loved Lazarus so much. And when he did what he was to do, calling him forth from the tomb, Mary intuitively knew that act of extravagant love would signal the end of the journey for Jesus.

So Mary leaves the kitchen and all its serving chores and goes to her bed table and brings out a special, costly ointment and proceeds to anoint the feet of Jesus, filling the dining room, beyond the aroma of the kitchen, with a pre-intuitive scent of burial.

Mary, having heard Jesus speak of his "glory," knew that this glory was not in being the guest at a festive banquet given in his honor. But what he did for the sake of love was the sign of her Lord's death. So with the ointment on his feet, mixed with her tears, she unclasped her hair and, using it as a sopping sponge, dried the ointment and tears, filling the room with death's aroma.

She knew what she was doing, and Jesus knew she knew. Judas, standing nearby, could contain himself no longer. He was heard to say, "What a waste!

Such a mindless extravagance! Who does she think she is? That ointment is worth a year's wages for a peasant. Think of what it would have meant for the poor."

Judas, quick with figures and the holder of the purse for Jesus and the disciples, actually was speaking not from the heart but out of how he would have apportioned such an amount for his own use.

Jesus, in John's Gospel, began his ministry at a banquet in Cana of Galilee. Then in Bethany, attending a dinner in his honor, his public ministry comes to a close.

This is a remarkable story. I find myself in the story. Are you not present also?

Am I Martha? At times I am: busy, hosting, doing things, greeting people, asserting words of caution, minding another's business, even when I'm unaware of the other's agenda.

Am I Mary? There are times when I have been: stepped aside from the normal flow, took a seat, listened, heard what was said, discerned what was meant, and did something spontaneously extravagant.

Am I Judas? O, yes, I have been: audacious in my reaction, quick to judge. How easy words of condemnation come to point out another's waste. Is it to cover my own greed? Why am I so annoyed by the extravagance of others?

This is a stewardship lesson. Let us do a Martha-Mary thing in sharing extravagantly of our adoration and generosity, whatever is ours to give.

11/8/98

Sermons for Special Occasions

"The cement of Christian commitment is hope, real hope — the hope that God can do through us what we cannot do for ourselves."

—Jon Appleton, 1981

Deacons: Do You, Therefore?

2 Timothy 2:15

Do your best before God, unto others and with no need for apology. As the Department of Transportation lays a straight road through the countryside, as the farmer plows a straight furrow through a field, as the mason cuts and squares a stone to fit in the structure of a building—do your best to lay a straight path through the truth.

Refuse to be lured down pleasant but irrelevant bypaths. Plough a straight furrow through the field of truth. Take each section of truth, as a stone, and fit it into its correct place. Allow no stone to usurp an undue place or an undue emphasis that would lean the structure of truth out of balance.

Your calling is God invoked; therefore, do your best. God does not call one whom God will not enhance, encourage, and inspire. Your calling is intended for service; therefore, do your best.

Open your eyes—not so much to what is but to what can be. Refrain from being an "is" person. Specialize in being a "becoming" person.

Open your ears to hear—not so much what is said but what is not said. You know certain people always talk, but listen. The talkers might actually say something. Also pay very close attention to the non-talkers. Listen to what is not being said. Sometimes silence is as loud as a bomb blast. You may find that the silence is more articulate than the prattle.

Use your eyes to see and your ears to hear. Jesus commands us to do so. But also open your hands to deeds of love and mercy.

Often the role of deacon has eroded to the level of supervision, management, custodial, official voice; we will not argue this status. However, the true measure of the deacon, biblically, is more in the line of a servant.

Jesus pointed his disciples to the fields and called upon them to see those fields, white unto harvest. Only opened hands can gather a harvest.

Jesus spoke in parables, often concluding his lesson with the words "Those who have ears, listen." Only opened ears can perceive truth and then gather the fruit. Your calling is to be unapologetic; therefore, do your best.

You have been called of God to a special service in the church. Unapologetically, look and listen, and have opened hands. Allow God to work through your eyes, in your ears, by your hands—to bring joy amid sorrow, peace amid conflict, hope amid despair, faith amid doubt, love amid neglect, and to effect the extraordinary amid what is ordinary.

Be aware of the danger of serving with a known expectation of the role of a deacon and of the expectation of yourself. Respond to the challenge to serve, not knowing where you are going.

A unique and exciting combination, which has never occurred before, will be ordained this hour: the "you" of whom you are and the role of deacon will merge. So here is the challenge: No person before or after is as you are. Therefore, stand tall, and do your best—imitating no other. Be yourself.

9/17/95

Epiphany: Time-conscious

Ecclesiastes 3:1-11

At the one-third mark of my fifty-seventh year, which coincides with the beginning of my seventeenth year as your pastor, I find myself drawn more and more toward the providence of God.

It is God who cares for us, who guides us, and who sustains us. Thankfully, God's providence is benevolent, a compelling grace of love even though by our merits God could choose to be vindictive.

The writer of Ecclesiastes, in search for meaning in life, observed, "God makes everything suitable for its time" (v. 11a).

This past week was my annual week to serve as chaplain at St. Mary's Hospital. I talked with people whom I had never known—patients and family members. I, being the chaplain, and they, because of special concerns, responded to the immediate time and its concerns.

I also talked with people whom I know well—patients and family members. On New Year's Eve afternoon I left the hospital quite in sadness yet with an overwhelming sense of gladness.

There is a time to be sad, and there is a time to be glad—and grace abounds when those times coincide. It is during such times that one is drawn to the providence of God—whose care prevails with the understanding that it is God "who has made us and not we ourselves" (Ps. 100:3).

In one room I found two daughters busy with their hands; one was writing and the other knitting. Both had keen ears for any different sound from their mother. I looked at their mother; it was her time to die. But in her dying moment I resurrected many glad times that she had lived in and through this community and church—caring, guiding, and sustaining us. She was a reflection of God's providence.

Certainly, sadness prevails for her, just lying there in her dying time. But just as surely, gladness erupts within to recall her living time when her voice was strong, her hands were active, her smile was broad, and her grace was abundant.

On my hospital sojourns I usually walk the stairs to the top floor, visiting rooms and working my way back down the stairs. On one hand, I need the exercise. There are 118 steps to the sixth floor at St. Mary's and 120 steps to the sixth floor at Regional.

On the other hand, I need the seclusion of the stairwells where I can catch my emotional and spiritual breath between floors. In almost every room I visit, I am compelled to act and react differently because of the existential moment. No two of us are alike, so our needs, reactions, emotions, and relations vary accordingly.

Indeed, there is "a time to weep, and a time to laugh; a time to embrace, and a time not to touch; a time to be silent, and a time to speak" (vv. 4-7). The writer of Ecclesiastes assays truly that each moment gives to us the adventure of significant action and reaction. He further found that God has "put a sense of past and future into our minds" (v. 11b).

Those daughters tending their mother were "on call" because of the blessed past. As their mother tended them as children, they were present to tend her as though she were their child. My feeling of gladness was having the past to recall her remarkable and gracious providence. And together we could anticipate a future where she would be released from her dying time to life eternal, where time is of no consequence.

I have always thought of the Wise Men as old men. Tomorrow is the day of Epiphany, the twelfth day following Christmas. It is a day to commemorate the coming of the Christ-child to the Gentiles, represented by the visit of the wise men from the East (Matt 2:1).

Epiphany deals with the finding of that which is of ultimate worth in ordinary circumstances, discerning the extraordinary among the ordinary. Often we note that those who have lived long help those who are younger to see life not in its broad sweeps but in its depth; not in its bright lights but in its quiet glow; not in its noise but in its hush; not in its achievements but in its calm.

I perceive that the wise men had lived their lives waiting to be led to that rendezvous in Bethlehem. And to have anticipated such a future moment in their past is a lesson for us to be time-conscious. What is our past teaching us about our future?

Would you be willing to follow an unusual star? Would you leave home, not knowing where you were going? Abraham, at seventy-five years of age, did. Moses, at eighty years of age, did.

God, according to Ecclesiastes, has given us a sense of past and future. Our past instructs us by the ways in which God cared for us, guided us, and sustained us. Likewise, our future will have the providential essentials wherever we may journey. We recall the past and dread not the future, for as God has been unto us, God will be to us—our source of care, our guide, and the one who will sustain us.

Granted, there are things that happen to us over which we have no control. However, if we are time-conscious, with our sense of the past and the future, there will be events and circumstances over which we can exercise control.

In the past what was true stood all tests, and what we honored proved significant. What was just prevailed, and what was pure was not defiled. What was lovely remained glorious, and what was gracious recalled delight.

No wonder Paul, in writing to the Philippians, cautioned them not to be time-conscious of earthly things but called upon them, saying, "Whatever is true, whatever is honorable, whatever is just, whatever is pure, whatever is lovely, whatever is gracious—think on such" (4:8).

1/5/92

Fathers' Day: Models of Love

Isaiah 41:4c, 6-7, 10b, 17, 20

Today is Father's Day. From a religious perspective we are to be commended in such a celebration. Such a day emphasizes the importance of the family and the father's role in the family. A father's greatest responsibility is not to succeed in his job, vocation, profession, or calling, but to be an example and a loving presence within the home.

G. Campbell Morgan's father gave him a verse of Scripture (Prov. 3:6) as a motto for life: "In all your ways acknowledge God and he will direct your paths." Morgan said, "After fifty years in the ministry, when I followed God's way, he kept his promises and directed my paths." The father of his birth and the Father of all creation were faith-stones upon which Morgan built his life.

A number of years ago two children, a daughter and a son of a former baseball superstar, went public about their father. The daughter said, "My father is the world's worst father," and the son spoke of their relationship being like a manager and player. He could not recall having been hugged or kissed, going on to say, "Even now (and he was in his twenties), I don't have his telephone number. I have to call his agent, and he tells my dad that I want to talk to him. We don't get in touch unless he wants to."

Such testimonies seem incredulous. However, and tragically so, such father-child relationships are not that unusual. Many are the examples of success-away-from-home / failure-in-the-home syndrome.

Today could be the begetting of new resolve in father-child kinships—a day to renegotiate our turf as fathers so that who we are in the world rings true with who we are in our homes. For children, today affords the occasion to pay respect by honoring our fathers, whether living or deceased. It is also, possibly, a brand-new day for mutual forgiveness, for the ways, true or biased, we fault one another in the disparities of our relationships.

Forgiveness recognizes wrongful turns in the past: lack of attentiveness, absenteeism from times that mattered, conduct unbecoming the hallmarks of honor, and harsh words of belittlement and strife. Many are the potholes in the road of a family.

To live day in and day out a family gets splattered by resolved and unresolved issues. So forgiveness does not come easily. And when it does come, it is through mutual acts of repentance.

Repentance is the act of turning toward one another, mindful of the discord, pain, and selfishness, but also of what is at stake. Time is too short to not move toward living beyond unresolved issues. That is precisely what occurred when the prodigal son came back home.

Life affords an expansive rearview mirror through which we see the good, the bad, and the ugly of the past. In the affairs of the family, in honoring our fathers, in affirmation of the home, today could be the proclamation of the good, the forgiveness of the bad, and the repentance of the ugly.

A survey in a recent report from a college in New York reveals that working mothers are not alone with feelings of guilt from being absent from their children. Fathers also carry a similar load of guilt. A new generation of fathers is emerging who do not want to repeat their fathers' absenteeism from their family memories. Stephen Segal, principal of Family Partners in Philadelphia, has noted that many fathers today are developing stronger bonds with their children than they knew from their own fathers.

A pause for realism is in order: The economic demands in today's society are so compelling that many parents feel they have no choice but to be in lockstep with their jobs. To provide the things necessary for a family does not leave much play for the average household. For a dad to call in and say to the boss "I can't be in today. I'm taking my sons on a picnic to the Sandy Creek Park" would be a radical stance—and one unlikely in accord with the expectations of a boss. However, to be unconditionally committed to our work is also a radical stance. To give all our energy, all our devotion, all our deliberations, all our thoughts, all our productivity into a consuming work schedule is to leave dangling the strings that bind a dad to his children and a husband to his wife.

It does, indeed, appear ridiculous for one to call in to work to announce an absence for a family outing. But it is also ridiculous to call home from work as a common occurrence to report absenteeism from home for the sake of work.

An American tradition has been to sentimentalize motherhood while viewing fathers as heroes. A teacher assigned the class to write a composition, and one boy wrote about his dad: "He can fight the strongest man, climb the highest tree, drive the fastest car, wrestle the biggest bear, and throw a football a mile. He can do almost anything. Mostly, though, he just takes out the garbage."

I have no problems viewing fathers as heroes. My dad was my hero. And I remember saying to my dad on the occasion of the death of Virginia's dad, "I lost the best friend I ever had."

Fathers in our households were heroes. They sacrificed for us. They provided abundance for us, but mainly in their rare ways they were models of love for us in the household. They placed demands upon us, some of which at the time seemed legalistic, binding, and confining. But in the long view we knew where they stood, and in our times of need they stood by us.

There was a time when I felt tied to a rope. Periodically, I tugged to break loose only to be yanked back into the yard. But one day when I tugged to be free, there was no tension from the other end, and all of the rope came coiling around my feet. As I looked back, my dad had a smile on his face, as though he were saying, "Okay, Jon, you're on your own—but you always know where home is."

When needy, unsure, and unsettled; when gasping for breath after a long, fruitless run; when absolutely exhausted—oh, the delight of going home again where a father home from work waits for us.

Oh, to be refreshed by one whose burdens are more than ours but whose shoulders bear yet our burdens, simply because he is our dad who does indeed wrestle bears and takes out the garbage and receives us into his arms.

Our hero! The one we turn to in our time of need.

6/16/96

Mother's Day: About Relationships

Psalm 139:1-8, 11-12, 13b-14a, 19, 23-24

Today is a special day. We call it Mother's Day, and for each of us it calls forth memories that only we can collect, which may be similar to the memories of others yet not like them at all.

If we have lived long enough to recall decades of memories, today is a day fraught with good thoughts and bad experiences; sunny days and stormy nights; pancakes, birthday cakes, and wedding cakes; youth and health; age and illness; independence and dependence; smiles and tears; times of help and times of hurt; joy and sorrow; life and death.

Mother's Day ricochets in my mind with multiple images of my mother, enjoined by two unforgettable Mother's Days. I recall embracing my mother on this day nine years ago, the day my dad died. Oh, the sorrow!

Then I recall watching my mother's delight seven years ago this day, the day my daughter married. Oh, the joy!

I have my thoughts on this day; they are strong, emotional, forever locked in—yet always germane for new perspectives. You have yours; thanks be to God!

This is not a day to be taken lightly. On one hand, there is much to celebrate, and the air of joyous celebration holds a rightful place. *Laughter* is a thought that comes to me when I think of my mother.

She is like the mother who wrote a note to her son's teacher: "Dear Mrs. Hawkins: If my Archibald is naughty, and he is on occasion, just punish the boy next to him. This would make quite an impression upon him and encourage Archibald to behave."

My mother possessed a cryptic, mischievous, intuitive type of humor. And even into her ninetieth year, her now-addled mind can still evoke laughter.

Introduction is a thought that comes to me when I think of my mother. As it was Timothy's mother, Eunice, and his grandmother, Lois, who introduced him to a faith that first lived in them, so it was for me. Though my dad was a minister, it was my mother to whom I went to ask of the faith that was first in her.

On one occasion my mother was called upon to introduce me to a women's group. She said, "You will note that Jon's name does not have an 'h' in it. His daddy and I, in naming him, sought to take all the 'h' out of him that we could."

Example is a thought that comes to me when I think of my mother. It was indeed the way she lived that was an example for me. But it was also in the things she pointed out to me in life, both to do and to avoid.

As I look back upon her influence, I recognize a precise legalism in my mother's portrayal of life. My mother and Judge Elbert Tuttle's mother were sisters of belief in the appeal of legalism, the safe haven of ethical conformity.

Judge Tuttle, a well-known jurist, made some courageous rulings on civil rights during the troubled days of segregation in Georgia. Upon retirement he was interviewed by the legendary broadcaster Walter Cronkite.

"Judge Tuttle," Cronkite said, "I understand you've never drunk whiskey."

The judge answered, "That's right, I've never in my life tasted an alcoholic drink."

Somewhat surprised, Cronkite asked, "Why not?"

The judge's reply was simple: "Because my mama told me not to."

Service is a thought that comes to me when I think of my mother. Paul admonished Timothy to "continue [to serve] in what you have learned and firmly believed, knowing from whom you learned it…from childhood" (2 Tim 3:14-15). There was a glad spirit in my mother's life as she cast forth her faith in words of witness and in deeds of service.

In the beginning I said that Mother's Day is not to be taken lightly—yet, on one hand, it has an air of joyous celebration. However, there is another side of this day's reality.

This day cannot be taken lightly, for there are many who find in it a recollection of pain; a memory better forgotten; and a thought that pervades the body, physically and emotionally, with fitful anxiety.

Consider the mother who has buried a child, experienced a miscarriage or a stillbirth; the woman who would have been an exemplary mother but could not be one for physical reasons; the one who has undergone an abortion or placed a child for adoption. Memory is not only recalling what has been but also thinking about what could have been.

Consider those, many of you, who have buried your mothers (and some most recently); those families alienated from one another; a stepmother who has not been a welcomed addition to the family circle; and a mother who is not awarded parental custody.

Mother's Day can be a day of wondrous acclaim for many while a time of tears, anxiety, and despair for others. Yet this day finds us together in a wide fellowship, sensing joy and sorrow, goodness and despair, light and darkness.

May all of us within this wide fellowship find the wonder of God's providence. May we experience not only God's gracious care of mothers and children, but God's tender concern for the barren and the orphan.

> Whether today I chuckle with laughter or groan in anxiety,
> > search me, O Lord.
>
> Whether today I fondly recall goodness or gloss over the hurt,
> > search me, O Lord.
>
> Whether today the spirit within me is alive or dormant,
> > search me, O Lord.
>
> Whether today I am confident in my love for others or reluctant to leave myself open,
> > search me, O Lord.
>
> For today, O Lord, is special, and I do not take it lightly.

5/11/97

Not Just Thanks-giving, but Thanks-living

John 14:15-31

Years ago, the great contralto Marian Anderson gave a concert in a small Nebraska college town. Afterward she returned to the hotel and approached the desk. She asked the young woman attending the desk if she had attended the concert. The young woman told the great artist that she was working her way through school and, therefore, was unable to attend the concert.

Then came an unforgettable moment: The world-renown singer stood in the hotel lobby, unaccompanied, and sang for the student "Ave Maria."

Ms. Anderson did not have to do that. But she did. Why? She knew what it was like to sit on the outside with the desire to be included. In 1939 she was refused permission to sing in Washington's Constitution Hall because she was black. But on Easter morning of that year, she sang outdoors at the Lincoln Memorial to an audience of 75,000. It was not until 1955 that she was to appear at the Metropolitan Opera.

Why did she sing for the college student? It was said that a sense of peace flowed through Marian Anderson and that she lived her life in thankfulness for the blessing she received and gave through her voice. She possessed that peace, not that the world gives, but that peace which the Lord had bestowed upon her.

It was said that her lifestyle was one of "thanks-living." Thanksgiving is much more than a holiday. Thanksgiving is an attitude that comes forth from a lifestyle of thanks-living.

Thanks-living is character in colorful display, like the awesome leaves of autumn. A thanks-living heart receives life's gifts and bestows life's dividends.

There are two lakes (called *seas*) in Palestine. One is fresh, and fish abound in it. Green grass adorns its shoreline. Trees spread their branches over it and stretch their thirsty roots into its damp soil. Along its shores children play and industry prospers.

Myriad streams and wadis flow into this lake from the springs and melting snow of Mt. Hermon. At its southern point the River Jordan takes the sparkling water of the Sea of Galilee (685 feet below sea level) some 70 miles, feeding into the Dead (Salt) Sea (1,290 feet below sea level, earth's lowest level).

Here, there is no splash of fish, nor grass or trees in sight, no playing children, and no prosperous industry. The air hangs heavy above the Dead Sea, high in humidity and intense in heat. What makes the difference?

The sea to the north receives, but does not keep, the flow of waters. The receiving and the giving are constant, as in thanksgiving. The sea to the south is shrewder, hoarding its income jealously. It will not be tempted into any generous impulse; every drop of water it gets, it keeps.

The Sea of Galilee receives, gives, and lives thankfully. The other, larger sea receives but keeps it all and is known as the Dead Sea. A thanks-living sea flows. A thanks-living heart lovingly embraces neighbor and God.

A seventh-century Eastern Orthodox mystic named Abba Dorotheus spoke of how the human desire to come nearer to God always brings us closer to one another. This "attribute of love," he said, reveals that the "closer our union with God, the closer is our union with one another also."

The foundational commandment from Scripture admonishes us to embrace God as the source of love and to embrace one another as the extension of love's intention. Such an embrace comes with the promised peace that the Lord gives and what the world can never provide.

A thanks-living heart is transformed. In Romans 12 we read: "I appeal to you therefore brethren, by the mercies of God, to present your bodies as a living sacrifice, holy and acceptable to God, which is your spiritual worship. Do not be conformed to this world, but be transformed by the renewal of your mind, that you may prove what is the will of God, what is good and acceptable and perfect."

The further removed we are from God, the more conforming we will be to the ways of the world and the more distant we will be from one another. The ways of the world can lead us to a distance far from the center—to a place of selfish ingratitude.

Thanklessness (ingratitude) keeps pretty rough company. Therefore, Paul advises us to turn our path toward the center, the embrace of reality, and away from the circumference of conformity. And as we move toward the center, toward embrace, toward God, we meet up with people who are both embracing and embraceable.

We encounter those whose minds are set by a transforming love. Thanks-living hearts are transformed and transforming hearts—becoming hearts that sing for an audience of one.

11/22/98

Sermons for Advent and Christmas

"The birth of Christ erases the consequences of past sin, enjoins the joy of each day, and anticipates the hope of the greater life which is yet to be."
—Jon Appleton, 1988

Resounding Hope

1 Thessalonians 3:1-13

When Timothy was sent by Paul to Thessalonica, it is stated that he was on a mission "to strengthen and to encourage" the Christians there "for the sake of their faith" (v. 2b). Actually, Timothy was sent because Paul was anxious as a parent about the welfare of the little church in Thessalonica, which he had established.

Paul was a hopeful warrior of the faith, but at times he was like an anxious father when separated from his children. Biblical hope can be defined as to cherish one's desire with anticipation, to trust, to be confident. Biblical despair (anxiety), contrary to hope, can be defined as to agonize in the fear of disappointment, to doubt, to be less than sure.

Paul found himself to have been overly anxious about the Thessalonians. Word has come of their persecutions and suffering at the hands of city officials, their exclusion from synagogue worship, and their own inner squabbles. So young were they in the faith, he allowed his anxiety for them to overextend his hope about them. He feared they might have lost the ball, and he was anxious about their defensive abilities. With the ball, many possibilities abound for success. Without the ball, much is the potential for failure.

When Timothy returned to Athens from Thessalonica, he came with good news of their "faith and love" (v. 6). Paul's response was to erupt into a marvelous prayer of hope—cherishing his cautious anticipation while dispelling his anxiety over their possible negligence.

Hope is one of the great expressions of biblical faith: "Now faith is the assurance of things hoped for, the conviction of things not seen" (Heb. 11:1). Or as the Williams New Testament puts it, "Now faith is the assurance of the things we hope for, the proof of the reality of the things we cannot see."

On this first Sunday of Advent, we have chosen hope—a cherished desire of our anticipation of the birth of Jesus—to be our theme. Ours is not a hope against hope, a feeling without any basis for expectant fulfillment; our hope is faith nurtured—the assurance that what we cannot see is as real as everything we do see.

In a sense it is more real than anything we do see, because all that we do see will pass away, but the fruition of our hope is eternal. With hope renewed, Paul rebounded. He got the ball back when Timothy told him the Thessalonians were strong in their faith and love. Their persecutions were real, as were their exclusions from worship and their inner squabbles. However, they were still in control—with the ball in their hands. Darksome are the troubles that step into the path of faith. So our hope must be ever resounding.

With hope renewed, Paul not only rebounded but *redounded*—which means to flow over. To rebound the ball is not the end; we are to keep the ball in play. Paul's key to a *redounding* faith was in his prayer life. Paul prayed about everything—much like my own dad before taking any trip.

Having his hope renewed, Paul shared with the Thessalonians his personal prayer life—his conversations with God, which included them. Have you ever considered letting someone you are praying for know you are praying for him or her?

God, through the prophets, let Israel know that one day God would come (advent) to them upon their behalf. Perhaps if we shared with those for whom we pray, they too might be better prepared for Christ's coming.

Paul's redounding lesson was this: Even in the simple, ordinary things of life, turn to God.

We know to do that. But life gets so crowded, so complex that we simply forget to include God in the venture. Now when a crisis comes, we call on God first.

William Barclay tells of a man who, with two others, began a yachting expedition on the west coast of Scotland. The man said, "When we are at home we hardly ever pay attention to weather forecasts, but when we were on the yacht we listened with all ears." It is quite possible to do without forecasts when life is comfortably safe; it is essential to listen when life is dependent upon them. God had come to Paul—an advent. Now Paul prayed that God would help him have an advent with the Thessalonians miles away. As a result, a hope so rebounding and so redounding erupts into resounding praise.

In the December 24, 1996, issue of *Upper Room*, Kermit Long of Arizona had a moving story about one Christmas Eve in Chicago:

> A gentle snowfall added to the already magical, mystical beauty of the season. I had just finished presiding over the first of our candlelight services. Rather than waiting in the church until the late hour for the second service, I visited in the hospital and roamed the few stores still open for late shoppers. I saw some people in a flower shop and joined them. Soon a young boy of about seven or eight came into the shop.

His clothes were torn, and his tennis shoes had holes in them. He walked purposefully over to the counter and asked the shopkeeper, "Do you have any rose for my mother for ten cents?" The man replied, "Wait just a moment and I'll see what we can do for you. On Christmas Eve, we have a special on roses for young fellows who want them for their mothers." Taking the lad's dime, he placed a dozen beautiful, long-stemmed red roses in his arms. With a big smile on his face, the boy left the flower shop and headed home. Those of us who looked on were warmed by what we had seen, and I know the shopkeeper felt the blessing of God for his generosity.

This busy, weary shopkeeper rebounded from the hectic stress of a long day and redounded into the true spirit of eternal hope. The minister who witnessed this transcendent moment, along with the other shop customers, sensed a resounding echo—"for unto us a child is born" who brings hope to eternal lives.

11/30/97

Jesus Christ: Light and Life

John 1:1-18

The experience of Jesus was an experience of God in John's Gospel. God is portrayed as both distant from and related to the world: beyond yet near; removed yet close. That God creates, provides, reveals, and redeems through the Word implies a distance between God and creation.

However, God also gives light and life by coming among us and "pitching his tent" in our camp (1:14). A classic formulation goes: God, not being identified with the world, can help us; God, being identified with the world, will help us.

The Gospel of John is a life message: "in him was life" (1:4); "Jesus is the Messiah, the Son of God, and...through believing you may have life in his name" (20:31).

Following his visit with Zacchaeus, Jesus exclaimed, "I have come that you might have life and life abundantly" (10:10). Now Zacchaeus was alive, and on the surface it would appear that he was doing well. He had a choice government position; he was protected by its orders; he was authorized by its mandates; he was untouchable.

But as a tax collector in a Jewish village, he was despised by his fellow Jews and ostracized by the Pharisees as a sinner. Even though he lived lavishly in his riches, he lived in isolation and, as his story reveals, with a guilt-ridden existence.

He was alive but not living. He possessed life's necessities and much more; as long as he made Rome happy, he prospered. Yet all that he possessed was not sufficient. Something was amiss.

Zacchaeus entertained Jesus in his home, but we know not the conversation that gave him new life. But we do know that Jesus, the bringer of life, gave to him the gift of living. Zacchaeus confessed as much when he revealed how he would start life anew: "Half my possessions, Lord, I will give to the poor; and if I have defrauded anyone of anything I will pay back four times as much" (Luke 19:8).

What is this life of which we speak? Are we not all alive? Jesus "pitched his tent" with us not as we view living but as he was alive.

Our living has a timetable, and we have the tendency to live disruptively and selfishly. We live with baited desires to outlive others; given the opportunity, we will use people as rungs on a ladder to rise to the top. We have weaknesses that allow other things to live our lives for us.

Strong-willed people allow alcohol to live for them. People of weak will allow an accuser to live for them. People of a codependent nature allow a self-seeking, self-serving user to live for them. People with uncontrolled desires allow money and its ceaseless yet never satisfying rewards to live for them.

Yes, multitudes are alive, ingloriously so, yet awash in living hells. Though living, Zacchaeus, despite all he had, was not alive. Then Jesus came, life itself. The life he offered Zacchaeus (and you and me) was not simply life that lasts forever. A life that lasts forever could be a terrible curse if a person's life is one from which he or she longs for release.

The good news of Jesus is that the life abundant is not measured by its duration but by its quality. How then do we, like Zacchaeus, enter into that life?

It sounds so simple—for many, too simple. But the Gospel of John throws it at us time and time again: "Believe in Jesus Christ!" Seventy different times in the twenty-one chapters, the appeal "to believe" occurs. But what does John mean by "to believe"?

Belief means the conviction of the mind that Jesus is God's Son. Look and behold him. Listen to him. Touch him. Learn from him. Study him. Think about him. Determine for yourself that he is or he is not who God says he is—who Jesus himself says he is—who Scripture says he is.

However, belief is more than a mind game. It is ultimately a trust—a will of the heart that his word is God's Word and that his commandments are to be binding.

Zacchaeus was alive, but it was not enough. So he chose to believe and to live abundantly. So can we.

Look at what's controlling you. Learn all about what you are living for. Study your daily living. Think about it. Determine for yourself if it's sufficient for all your needs.

Take your time, but don't waste time. The giver of every good and perfect gift, including life itself, awaits your belief.

12/01/96

Upon Being Ready

Matthew 24:36-44

Two little girls were looking with their mother at a nativity scene displayed in a department store window. Shepherds were kneeling to the side, and a variety of barnyard animals were present. Behind the rustic manger fluffed with straw stood Joseph.

Mary was bending attentively over the manger bathed in an aura of light. As the mother bid the girls to hurry on, the younger girl whispered to her sister, "They forgot to put the baby Jesus in the manger."

A story is told of a rabbi in Greenville, South Carolina, who was accustomed to questioning the values of society by telling his children, "That's fine for everyone else, but it's not fine for you. You are special. You are a Jew. You are different, with a different story, a different set of values."

In light of our culture's takeover of Christmas, making of it a spectacular holiday, it is time for Christian parents to say to their children, "What others do may be fine for them, but you are special. You are different. You are a Christian. A filled stocking on the mantle has some kinship with the Christmas story, but it's minimal in comparison to the presence of the Christ-child in the manger."

In the world Christmas is observed as a holiday, but in the epic story of salvation Christmas is a holy day. A holiday is a day off, a break, a time for ourselves. A holy day is an adventure, an occasion for readiness, a time to stand in awe.

Christmas has been orchestrated as a time to do for others what we want them to do for us in a self-serving manner. To cover all sides, we stockpile reserve gifts should an unexpected donor appear. Gift-wrapping entrepreneurs make millions of dollars on paper, tissue, and ribbon that become instant trash. In a normal family's post-giving cleanup, the cost of the wrapping materials, sacked as garbage, could feed a needy family indefinitely.

In a normal family's post-Christmas-dinner clean-up, the amount of food left over and often thrown away would be a mind-boggling feast for a street family. We expend untold energy, time, and money in travel costs, decorations, food purchases, and gift buying to be ready for Christmas.

Is such expenditure wrong? No, not necessarily—unless it depletes our energy for holiness or consumes our time for the holy moment or we spend everything on ourselves to the exhaustion of what Christmas is all about.

Author Philip Yancey locked himself in an isolated cabin one mid-winter just to read through the Bible. He came away with an unusual discovery that the storyline of the Bible is not about moral laws, divine dictums. Rather, the Bible is romance, following progressively the story of God as "the jilted lover."

God, the humiliated, becomes God the Father of the Christ-child. How can we not get ready, unreservedly, for so wondrous a gift?

Together, let us resolve the child's place in the manger. However others may choose to spend Christmas, let us underline how special it is. It is a different day, like none other. It is the grandest storyline of all times.

Let us prepare as the one working in the field who felt the wind of the Spirit moving through the brush and be lifted into the rhythm of the ages. Let us prepare as Noah, mindful of God's hints for sustenance though the world around us is consumed by its make-believe ardor.

Let us major upon being ready.

12/3/95

John, the Forerunner

Luke 3:1-20

According to prophetic tradition, one was to come as a forerunner to announce that the one who was to come was coming. Isaiah put it this way:

> The voice of one crying out in the wilderness: "Prepare the way of the LORD, make his path straight. Every valley shall be filled. And every mountain and hill shall be made low, and the crooked shall be made straight, and the rough ways made smooth; and all flesh shall see it together, the salvation of God, for the mouth of the LORD has spoken." (40:3-5)

These words were spoken some six centuries before the birth of Jesus. These were excitable, positive words spoken dramatically though clouded in mystery to evoke hope. They were words spoken to a people who had lost everything—their structure as a nation, their institutions for worship, their land, their possessions, and their identity.

These words address a theme basic to both Jewish and Christian theology: that God is present in the affairs of human history.

Each of the four Gospels includes this prophetic utterance to introduce John the Baptist as the forerunner of Jesus. John's station in the affairs of God is not to be taken lightly nor mentioned fleetingly. His was an ancient voice with a new tension; an odd demeanor with an alluring appeal; a strange presence with a chilling reverberation, calling for a decisive decision with a timeless guarantee.

Yes, it was in his voice that echoed from the banks of the Jordan into the hills of Judah, up the valley of Jezreel to the ascending slopes of Galilee and unto the coastal plains of the Mediterranean. His message spread—compelling fishermen and farmers, merchants and maidens, soldiers and scribes.

Pharisees and Sadducees, the poor and the prosperous came to the Jordan valley to hear that voice—persuasive in tone, precise in judgment, and precious in promise. Seeing John in person caused the people to think of the past.

Whispers from those who had heard him and the gossip of those going to hear him spoke of the wild vagabond prophet Elijah, who like John came from the wilderness. They asked, "Is he Elijah sent by God?" "Or Moses?" they may have asked while looking across the Jordan to the distant reaches of Mt. Nebo from which Moses viewed the land of promise.

John was on stage with all of Israel's history as his backdrop. Yet his was not a recitation of Israel's glory years but a voice urging them to look within themselves.

Charles Sherer, in the mid-1950s, said, "The road to tomorrow leads through yesterday." And John came as yesterday's charade to parade tomorrow's hope. John's futurism was to be not in yesterday's glory but in tomorrow's glory. It is a future akin to the promises of yesteryear but linked to a person about to come.

This rugged individualist came upon the scene to set the stage for God's new age. John was the chosen man to announce the man chosen to be Israel's future. His birth, improbable because of the age of his parents, Zechariah and Elizabeth, came to be the providence of God's presence and promise.

John was a man of strength, morals, and courage. Imposingly, he stood at Jordan's banks, and the people missed not a word. But his words were words of introduction. He could move a crowd, woo an audience—but not unto himself. His was a message of introduction.

He made profitable for consideration Isaiah's old prophetic hymn about valleys being lifted to plains, mountains being leveled, hills being scaled down, crooked lanes being made straight, rough ways being made smooth. For generations people had sung the tune and recited the words—though hope had dimmed and faith diminished.

Now John comes thundering down Jordan's valley shouting, screaming, chiding, and causing the people who had hope to take hope. His task was to be a presence "to turn" the people onto a level field. It was a generation of crooked ways and rough places. It was a time of terrible terrain for one to find his or her footing.

But John said, "Those of you in the valley will be lifted up (hope). Those of you in your mountain aeries will be brought down (judgment). Behold, one will come in whose presence none of us will be worthy to tie his sandals, but he will come and touch the most diseased of us. He will teach the most obtrusive of us and will train the most humble of us."

He comes as the One promised of old. His field will be level: "Whosoever believes" (John 3:16).

Sure enough, he who was to come, did come. And John said of him, "Behold, the Lamb of God, who takes away the sin of the world! This is he of whom I said, 'After me comes a man who ranks before me'" (John 1:24-30).

Yesterday's voice, the forerunner, acclaimed tomorrow's hope—the "Lamb of God!"

12/7/97

Wonder, Ponder, and Adore

Luke 2:1-20

From Scripture we note a marked contrast between Herod the king and Jesus the king. King Herod reacted with force to the threat of another king, as he called out his troops to murder innocent boys in a given region. King Jesus expressed his royalty so differently.

Jesus, who was the King of Kings, assumed the air of a peasant. He dined with publicans and openly talked with harlots. To his coronation he rode a donkey. He was a king who served, the Lord who came alongside.

Flannery O'Connor once wrote a short story titled "A Good Man Is Hard to Find." The primary character is a decadent man named "Misfit." Continually, Misfit does evil yet understands the concept of justice and punishment. What he cannot comprehend is mercy. What Jesus taught about the relationship between justice and mercy is beyond his grasp.

At one point in O'Conner's story, Misfit shouts his frustration, "Jesus throwed everything off balance! Jesus throwed everything off balance!"

That's one way of saying it. Another more sophisticated but less memorable way would be, "Jesus shatters our assumptions." Jesus meets so many of our assumptions head-on—and he broadsides our ways of thinking and establishes new and different possibilities.

When the shepherds came to the manger, they told everyone what they had been told by the angel. And all who heard their report "wondered" at what they heard.

Mary, the mother of Jesus, in hearing the shepherd's story, "pondered" every word in her heart.

When the shepherds left, returning to their flocks, they did so "glorifying and praising God for all they had heard and seen, as it had been told them." To experience the wonder and to ponder the story elicits praise and adoration.

Jesus was indeed to be an unusual king. The role of a king was entrenched in Jewish history. In Old Testament literature a common title for God is *king*: "The Holy One of Israel is our king" (Ps. 89:18).

King David became the prototype of an expectant messianic king. In Matthew's Gospel the Magi come with the question, "Where is he who is born king of the Jews?" (v. 2:2).

When Jesus entered Jerusalem for the last time, he was acclaimed with the shouts, "Blessed be the king who comes in the name of the Lord" (Luke 19:38). On his cross it was inscribed, "This is Jesus, the King of the Jews."

What do we assume about a king? What images come to mind? We don't run into kings all that much, so we latch onto history and literature for our images.

A king is a male ruler over others, one who demands and expects obedience and submission. A king exerts power to protect his kingdom against enemies, providing order for his subjects. His power may be benevolent, or it could be abusive. Either way, the power of dominion over his subjects clearly rests with the king.

What about King Jesus? Jesus says "No!" to our assumptions about kingship. He shatters the forms of our concepts: "Jesus throwed everything off balance!"

As he began his ministry, we hear his "No!" during the temptations in the wilderness. The people expected a messiah who would be a warrior-king, one who would smash their enemies and mount a throne of power.

So that subtle voice of temptation whispered, "Be king! All the kingdoms of the earth could be yours." But Jesus said, "No!"

After feeding the 5,000 some wished to draft him to be king, whether he was willing or not. But Jesus insisted, "No!"

His enactment of royalty was so "off balance"—alien to expectation and hope, ridiculous by worldly measure, and counter to the assumptions of history and prophecy. All authority was his in heaven and on earth, and he botched it. Even in his dying moments on the cross, with mocking horseplay and teasing gestures, it was shouted, "If you are king of the Jews, come down from the cross and we will believe in you" (Matt. 27:42).

They assumed, as we often do, that a king is overpowering, forceful, and capable of leaping buildings and defying death. Jesus was different. So they laughed at him as he bled to death.

Turn to the electronic church and the swelling numbers of fundamentalists today and discover that the assumptions that ran counter to the kingship of Jesus still abide and wax well. Authoritarian religion is an avalanche motion: power over justice, submission over mutuality, blind obedience over questioning faith, order over love, dependence over independence.

Amazingly, such authoritarianism in religion (and politics) is appealing in our day. "No! No! No!" says Jesus to such authoritarian expression. He refused to be that kind of king. He recoined kingship radically.

This is the difference: Royalty to Jesus meant not the power of force, but the power of self-giving love. He exposed the fatal flaw of force—namely, it cannot conquer the heart. Force can achieve submission, but it cannot elicit love.

God is love. So it should have been expected that his Son would have been a lover, not a coercer.

We are made in God's image, and our hearts yearn to love and to be loved. Love cannot be coerced—every parent knows that. So Jesus, God's Son of love, came as a king unlike any known or expected.

By preference another type of king would have been our choice: one who would rule over history and make everything work out to our advantage; one who speaks audibly to a select messenger so he could tell us what to believe and what to do; one who keeps law and order; one who would erase mystery, eliminate agony, and blot out suffering. But those are not the kingly traits of Jesus.

In Jesus, God lays aside the crown and the robe and the sepulcher and assumes the power of the towel and the basin, the power of a wooden cross, the power of a father awaiting a prodigal son, the power of an empty tomb.

Even at his birth those who heard the shepherds' story "wondered." And of those things that Mary kept in her heart, she "pondered." And as the shepherds returned to their flocks, a joy overwhelmed them as they "adored" Jesus the baby king.

This Jesus—who "throwed everything off balance"—is indeed King of Kings and Lord of Lords.

12/18/88

God Is with Us

Matthew 1:18-25

There is much about the whole religious enterprise that seems superannuated and irrelevant. But that is not so when we come to Christmas. Jesus, the Christ, is born. He is born among beasts whose bittersweet breath infiltrates a stable's stench, and nothing is ever the same again.

Christmas is a strange event—a new day, a precious moment. Those who believe can never be sure of God again. Forever and forever, God cannot be "pigeonholed." Once we visit the stable, we can never be sure where or when God will next appear.

We can never be sure to what lengths God will go to be near us, nor to what depths God will come to find us. Our paths may cross in the strangest places.

God having met us at a stable makes no place ill suited for yet another rendezvous. At that stable, holiness and power and majesty were present in the apparent inauspicious birth of a peasant's child. There is no place or time so lowly or earthbound but that holiness, power, and majesty may not be present.

Religion has the tendency, with time, to designate certain places as "*the* places," to specify certain people as "*the* people," to glorify certain days as "*the* days," and to qualify certain creeds as "*the* creeds." As humans we are much more comfortable in qualifying our religion. By so doing, we feel safer.

We go to great lengths to register religion in the black-and-white columns. But at the stable God blew to smithereens our compulsion to specify molds whereby faith comfortably fits. At the stable God's Son was born naked into a world that toils to clothe itself in prescribed robes of self-righteousness.

Being birthed in such a place, at such a time, and in such a manner shouts to the avowed cynic and the would-be faithful, "There is no place nor time nor way whereby you can hide from God nor whereby God will hide from you!"

We may think we can post signs like "No room in the inn," but when we rise the next morning to jog around the parking lot, God is there by the kennel in the beam of a glorious light surrounded by the paperboys and the computer executives from up East.

God is most strong, most present, and most majestic when appearing to be most helpless. And who is more helpless than a newborn babe?

Where we least expect God to be, God comes most fully. Every tree and tinsel, every poinsettia and program, every Christmas card and Christmas carol, every present and pastry are signs reading "No room in the inn" unless they are avenues by which we are led to the stable to meet the God who is in Christ reconciling us unto himself.

How seriously we are compelled to celebrate Christmas. Nothing is ever the same again!

I'd rather not be this serious; how about you? Let's mold our own Christmas and slip the real one under the rug; let's designate places and keep them holy; let's glorify certain days and keep them holy; let's qualify a creed and keep it holy. It will be so much more comfortable for us to avoid a God who might show up in unseemly places.

No. Let us reaffirm ours as a faith that is appropriate and meaningful—one whereby the "God who comes" will be the "God to whom we want to come."

Our ways are not God's ways. In choosing to meet us upon our turf, God is apt to meet us in a stable or in an ICU unit or in the setting sun or under an ice-laden tree. It is our turf, but it is Christ's birth—and it's all mystery.

To me the most haunting words of the Bible are, "For *unto you* is born this day." Yes, "unto you" is the watchword of one who loves us so much that we are apt to meet God at any time, any place—even now, even here.

12/20/98

Christmas Eve: A Poem

He was born, as prophets foretold,
Whose origin predated time.
Symbols, like lights, lit the night
O'er the place of birth consigned.

The hushed mystery of that night
Enticed both humans and kine.
Seeing him born of humble state
Mattered not to those who would find

The little boy "in swaddling clothes"
Mary's son, God's sign
Of a love in pursuit of hearts,
The light forever to shine.

He was born long, long ago,
God's only "so beloved" design,
To extend to the likes of you and me
A second birth, new life to find.

Yes, the little boy was born on earth
That we could be borne to heaven's clime.

—Jon Appleton 12/24/94

Tomorrow! Oh, Tomorrow

A Christmas Eve Meditation
Isaiah 35:1-10

While God was being born, the world was quite busy doing its thing. Its "thing" was a new thing: that all the world was being registered (at least all the male world).

Tourist agents were beside themselves. Caravan and camel rental agencies were overbooked. They were down to renting donkeys. Elitist customers were disgruntled, having been enjoined by the lowliest of people, traveling in all directions from every city, town, village, and crossroad—each going to his "own town" (the seat of ancestral birth).

The inns were overbooked. The whole world was in movement. Coinciding with this universal registration was some type of imposed taxation precisely at the time the Son of God was born.

Joseph, a carpenter from Nazareth in Galilee, accompanied by Mary, who was expecting her first child (though there was hush-hush about that reality since they only "publicly intended" to be married), made the pressing, importunate journey to Bethlehem in Judea, a few miles south of Jerusalem. The overall travel distance was similar to a trek here in Georgia from Athens to the Atlanta airport.

Why would she, in her condition, make such an arduous journey? She was not required to go. It was a man's world. Emperor Augustus' decree addressed the male populace only.

The writer Luke allows a lot of space between his lines, leaving us to wonder and to suppose. So very much had transpired leading toward the birth of God's Son. An angel had appeared to Mary and told her strange and wondrous things about being found in God's favor.

Mary knew the purity of her own heart as well as the purity of her body. Yet the angel spoke to her about the power of the Holy Spirit "overshadowing" her and that she would conceive a child who would be "holy"—God's Son.

An angel had also confided with Joseph, who learned of Mary's pregnancy before he had known her in marriage. Being a righteous man, he was unwilling to publicly expose Mary and, therefore, had planned to discreetly dismiss her.

But when the angel revealed the story of Mary's privilege, he was reminded of a passage in Isaiah: "Look, the virgin shall conceive and bear a son, and they shall name him Emmanuel" (7:14).

Emmanuel means "God with us." Thus, in Bethlehem of Judea a peasant woman from Nazareth in Galilee, in the company of her carpenter husband-to-be, gave birth to God's Son.

The movement of the world was an intentional ploy by Caesar Augustus to precisely name every citizen and locate each household. It was a ploy to harness allegiance, to place upon them the yoke of a subject people, and to set the boundaries of identity and confinement.

While Caesar was having his way with a captive populace, the world's first citizen, God himself, gave to the world a baby named Jesus, born to unharness the things of the world that bind, limit, and forestall. A generation later this Jesus, whose name means salvation, announced his mission with these words: "I have come to set the captive free" (Luke 4:18).

Had we been in charge of the birth of Jesus, we would have made his coming spectacular, trying to respect his true identity as the Son of God. His birth would have been in a palace, a king's domain—palatial, ostentatious, opulent, plush—to reflect the splendor of his origins.

Or his birth would have been in one of the great commercial seaport cities of the world so the news of his coming would have been "the news" in every port of call around the Mediterranean and beyond.

Or his birth would have occurred in an established religious community that projected his coming as a present reality of a futuristic hope.

However, when God moved in, it was a silent night, bestirring only a few ordinary people who were let in on the decree that paled Caesar's degree. Caesar sought to find and to confine that which God, in Jesus, sought to reveal: self-giving love that finds all people and sets them free.

What a night it was! And what a tomorrow it was to be!

Don't you just love the way God's act is put together—its audacious simplicity, its discreet announcement, its improbable actors, its backstage performance, its one shining star, its barnyard effect?

Don't you just love the heroes and the heroine? Was there ever a man taller than Joseph, who when he knew the whole story would not forsake Mary for a single moment?

Was there ever an audience so enthralled, yet responsive as the shepherds in the fields? Could angels ever have sung more gloriously? Could the animals ever have been so quiet and docile?

And then Mary—so blessed of God; so bound to Joseph; so tossed, yet so pliable; so far from home, yet so at home; so ecstatic, yet listening—pondering and storing everything in her heart.

And then Jesus—so very human, yet so very God. Emmanuel—God with us. Why would we ever let the things going on in the world vie for tomorrow?

Tomorrow! Oh, Tomorrow. God is with us!

12/24/95

The Child, His Authority

A Christmas Day Meditation
Isaiah 9:2-7

We have all heard litanies of oxymorons—contrary combinations of words like *jumbo shrimp, long shorts, fresh frozen, pretty ugly, holy war,* and *inactive Christian.* However, one of the more interesting oxymorons is this: *Silent Night.*

Christmas Eve, even for those of us who attended the candlelight service, was anything but a silent night. Last-minute shopping is clamor personified. You who are holiday chefs preparing today's feasts spent yesterday with the clatter, rattle, and dinging of dishes, pans, and pots.

Families congregating, thankfully, never do so in silence. It is household NOISE, capitalized.

However, the world's most popular Christmas carol is "Silent Night." Why? Why such an oxymoron?

We love to sing "Joy to the World," but we'd rather sing "Silent Night." We join heartily to sing "O Come, All Ye Faithful," but we'd rather sing "Silent Night." We enjoin in awed hushness to sing "O Little Town of Bethlehem," but we'd rather sing "Silent Night."

Is it because everything about Christmas is an oxymoron? Christmas celebrates the birth of a little baby boy named Jesus—while at the same time it is the celebration of the coming of the divine messianic king, the Lord of Lords.

It is the combinations of opposites that make Christmas mysteriously true. Jesus is the divine Son of God, yet human. Jesus is the baby, little—yet the ruler, huge.

There is so much to Christmas—as though all of life is wrapped within the silence of the universe, amid the inky darkness of night.

There is so much wrapped up in Christmas that to simply hear it would be too awesome or to simply see it with human eyes would be too amazing.

Jesus was born as Counselor. How unlike an image of God as a ruthless judge who takes an eye for an eye and a tooth for a tooth.

Jesus was born as Almighty God. How unlike an image of God as one far away, remote, and aloof.

Jesus was born as Everlasting Father. How unlike an image of God as a demanding, absentee landlord.

Jesus was born as Prince of Peace. How unlike an image of God as one who abides in heaven's peace while leaving us to struggle on earth amid conflict, strife, envy, and vengeance.

Therefore, out of a "silent night" came just enough sound for our ears to hear and just enough light for our eyes to gradually get accustomed to who this baby is and to what this baby will grow up to be all about.

Tucked into the holy pages of Scripture are two images so frighteningly opposed that bringing them upon the same stage would be disastrous. There is the lion, the king of the jungle, whose roar brings fright, whose nearness evokes anxiety. Then there is the lamb, the scapegoat upon the altar, whose bleat denotes fright and whose nearness means the shedding of blood as the sacrificial lamb.

However, out of the drama of "silent night," Jesus is as one the lion of Judah and the lamb to be slain on the altar. But note what this baby will do as the lion: he will look upon the lamb not as prey to devour but as innocence to embrace. And as the lamb he will look upon the lion not as pursuer to flee but as strength to embrace. In Jesus the lion and the lamb will lie down together, even as Isaiah foretold.

This child who was born in darkness is the light of the world. Together, we sing "Silent Night" on cue each year so we might accustom our ears and eyes to the wonder of beholding so great a salvation.

God in Christ became one of us so we might become one like him—which is the most significant oxymoron of all. He lived, to die, so that we might live.

"Silent Night, Holy Night" dispels the fright as we see the sight of the star so bright.

12/25/94

Sacrifices, Gifts and Presents

Luke 2:22-40; Romans 12:1-8

"What did you get for Christmas?" That's a popular way of beginning a conversation this time of the year—especially when relating to children.

At Christmastime a lot of attention is given to presents. Much is said about the person who receives a present by what the present is.

Virginia and I have a nephew, Jon Appleton Massey, who loves to be outdoors—hunting, fishing, and boating. Jon's mother, Virginia's sister, suggested that this year he be given presents for his student apartment in Macon. One present we gave Jon was a set of placemats with wildlife duck scenes imprinted upon them.

As the family gathered to open gifts, I watched Jon from across the room. It was a rather long, flat box—wrapped beautifully—that he slowly attacked as though apprehensive. Opening the box and spreading the tissue, his eyes glowed momentarily as he raised each mat, noting the various scenes.

But here's what I saw in Jon's eyes: As good as this is, I'd rather have had a decoy or waders or at least a duck-labeled shirt or pants. After opening all his presents, he sought Virginia and me out with a proud smile—showing us what our daughter Catherine had given him.

Our present to him was what Jon needed—according to his mother. But the present really didn't fit because it was not Jon; he preferred the real thing.

A present is more than a present; it is the announcement of a perception. It symbolizes biography, even autobiography. For the giver it is a symbol of the recipient in my mind, how one perceives him or her. For the recipient it is how one appears to the giver.

With this background I would like for us to look at three words as post-Christmas thoughts: presents, sacrifices, gifts. We usually talk about people *giving* presents, *making* sacrifices, and *using* gifts.

At the time Jesus was born, Jewish people would make sacrifices of animals and agricultural produce upon altars to God. We read of this in Luke 2:22-24. As a part of the ritual for circumcision, when Jesus was eight days old, a pair of pigeons were killed by the priest at the altar. Then they were completely consumed by fire.

The pigeons were sacrificed utterly to God in a way that no one else could derive any benefit from them. The sacrifice was for God alone. Therefore, one *makes* sacrifices.

The apostle Paul, when writing to the Romans (12:6-8), spoke of the gifts we possess by grace. He referred to gifts as talents, skills, or qualities that have been given to us and which we are obliged to use. Therefore, one *uses* gifts.

Now, presents are those things given for others to use. Presents are essentially material things, but as we have previously noted, they often symbolize the identity of the recipient as well as the giver's perception of the recipient. Therefore, one *gives* presents.

Recalling the birth of Jesus, let us weave these words together. Jesus was God's present to us. In receiving Jesus as God's present (John 3:16), we actually look into a mirror and behold him in light of what we can become as children of God (John 1:12).

As we behold this wondrous present given to us, we note his marvelous gifts in "going about doing good" for others. His talents, such as teaching, were used to bring clarity to old laws, to bring acceptance of all people, and to bring inclusion of all nations. His skills, such as healing, were used to open the eyes of the blind, to open the ears of the deaf, and to open the tombs of the dead.

His qualities, such as compassion, were used to dine with sinners, to call tax collectors, and to die between two thieves. He sanctioned the *use* of his gifts in these words: "Do unto others as you would have them do unto you."

Looking into the mirror of God's wondrous present to us, we are commissioned to *use* our gifts in this same spirit.

Jesus lived and died sacrificially. He came to serve and to make of himself a sacrifice for our sins. Thus is introduced a radical reversal in relation to Jewish tradition.

Yes, Jesus gave himself utterly to God. But he sacrificed himself utterly for us as well. When Jesus presented himself to the will of his Father, that will was to give himself upon our behalf.

Thus, we no longer bring pigeons to the altar or bulls or wheat to be consumed by fire. We do not bring death to the altar. Death has already been served.

"The wages of sin is death; but the gift of God [the sacrifice of Jesus] is eternal life through Jesus Christ, our Lord" (Rom. 6:23). That is why Paul admonished us to be "living sacrifices."

Before Jesus, sacrifice meant death. In Jesus, sacrifice meant death. But now for us, the recipients of God's gift of Christ, sacrifice means to live. We are to live utterly to God.

Now that Christmas Day has passed, let us remember that we *give* presents to others for their benefit and as a symbol of their identity. We *use* our gifts for the good of others. And we offer ourselves as "living sacrifices" to God—to become instruments of God's mercy, peace, and love.

If we consciously do this latter thing, live sacrificially, the other two things, giving presents and using our gifts, will be built upon the foundation of God's will as well.

12/29/91

God's Boy and Bess, Oh Bess

John 1:14

As children of the light, one and all,
With wonder we had gazed upon the infant boy.
Though many a detracting light befell us all
His Light still shone better than our grandest toy.

Seated with immediate family and kin around the sparkling tree,
We opened gifts, bound in wondrous wrappings, with cries of special joy;
Yet amid the family's gala treats of presents given so free,
No gift could outshine God's Son for the darkness he came to destroy.

At the noon hour on that Christmas Day, still chanting about our gifts,
Mom called us to the tables laden with the season's feast.
Dad recited the traditional yule prayer, which soared our hearts to lift
the cares which often beset us—from the eldest to the least.

The turkey, though a bit tough, was edible, drowned in gravy;
And the ham had a wondrous flavor wedged amid vegetables too, too many.
With a twinkle in my eye I winked at Grannie dearie
For in all the many servings—green beans there were not any.

And wonder of wonder, to my delight yeast rolls had risen to the occasion;
And when we had eaten much more than enough, far, far beyond calories, so,
    so many,
Then to our ears came that expectant call to attend the dessert procession.
Would it be ambrosia and chocolate, or caramel, or coconut cake?
Or would we lie and say, "We don't want any!"?

Afternoon came, and the children fled to the yard; but the ladies with energy
    moved to the kitchen
With stacks and stacks of dirty dishes, while the men folk appeared drowsed
    and listless.
A wondrous time had been had by all until at the hour around dusk,
With the year's most wondrous day well spent, shouts went out, "Where is
    Bess?"

Bess, oh Bess, a child of just four was e'er so young, yet so rare;
With a cadence to her own beat and an abstractness beyond her peers.
It was not unusual for her to play with contentment, and with others share;
While at other times she had been known, just out of the blue, to disappear.

A note of anxiety swept across the family, for darkness was minutes away;
And Bess, oh Bess, did not respond at all, even to the calls of her brother, Clay.
Soon neighbors, responding to the alarm, joined in the hunt for treasured Bess.
Around the small village men and boys searched and searched, even beyond the hill's crest.

Bess, oh Bess, was not to be found as the search extended into darkness.
There arose worry on frowning brow, with not a few thoughts of hopelessness.
The search widened as folk arrived from farms, far and near,
While her dad and mother fought to control their tears.

The Baptist church was on the outskirts of the village;
and the fellowship hall was designated as the rendezvous place.
Neighborhood ladies brewed coffee and took stations to serve leftover Christmas cakes and pies.
So when midnight came and still no Bess, Pastor Jones was asked to say grace.

He stood to pray, but said not a word, though all heads were bowed.
Then in a whisper he asked everyone to follow him into the sanctuary to pray.
Without a word being spoken, one and all followed as though in tow
And moved down the aisle toward the pulpit as Preacher Jones led the way.

He said after a moment, "Let us pray," and with words fit for ole Jeremiah,
He called upon God's mercy that we would find that little girl, loved by all.
Grown men dabbed tears from their eyes, and little children stood still by mamas.
The risen words of prayer filled the chancel, and then quietness, like a net, fell o'er all.

The assembly of friends and neighbors by the prayer's "Amen" did not stir for quite a while
And then with new resolve turned to start the search anew.

But someone whispered, "Attention!," pointing to the crèche; and little Bess
    with a sleeping smile
Was laying at the foot of the manger and Mary and Joseph and the animals
    too.

Bess' dad yelped with joy, and her mother broke into tears,
Startling Bess, oh Bess, into confused wakefulness.
Her dad held her up in his arms, crushing her at times to his chest, amid
    cheers.
And all the anxieties and fears vanished into joyous hugs and caresses.

When the atmosphere fell into a more normal order, Bess' mother chided her
    little daughter,
Asking her in front of everyone why she had wandered away from all of us.
And Bess, with the wonder only children can exhibit, responded,
"I'm sorry, Mom, but I so wanted to spend his first night with baby Jesus."

While I had been thinking earlier that day that indeed Jesus, the infant boy,
was grander, so much more than all our toys, It was Bess, oh Bess, whose own
    infant mind
had discerned the season's ultimate joy—to spend her time with the little boy.
And so our family and village friends found at Christmas midnight, that the
    alarms and stresses of life
find peace at the feet of God's Son of Light—the little Jesus boy.

12/29/96

Communion Meditations

"Jesus frees us to be borrowers from God. And his first offer is that we borrow what we need most: forgiveness of our sins."
—Jon Appleton, 1990

Freed From Hiding

Isaiah 50:4-9

A student once asked Carlyle Marney, "Dr. Marney, where was the garden of Eden?" Marney answered, "215 South Elm Street in Knoxville, Tennessee."

"Ah, c'mon, you're kidding me," replied the student. "It was somewhere in the Middle East, wasn't it?"

"Well, you couldn't prove it by me," said Marney, "for it was on Elm Street, when I was a boy, that I stole a dime out of my mama's purse and went down to the store and bought candy and ate it. Then I was so ashamed that I ran back home and hid in the closet. It was there my mama found me and asked, 'Why are you hiding? What have you done?'"

Three things Marney's lesson teaches us: Each of us must locate our own Eden where we (1) first betrayed our highest selves; where we (2) discovered that there was a shadow-side within us, and that we (3) tried to hide from the reality of our duplicity.

It does not matter whether we know the precise location of the garden of Eden or not. However, it is significant that what happened to Adam and Eve is the story of us all.

When God came looking for Adam and Eve and called them by name, God indicted them for their sinful act. Yet the fact that he "came, calling" them also indicated that he would not abandon them.

That theme of "coming, calling" is the bottom line of the entire biblical story.

Isaiah spoke of it as "The Lord GOD opened my ear." In the "coming, calling" God, he found help, unashamedly.

It is with opened ears and opened eyes that we come out of hiding to the Lord's table in obedience to Jesus, who "came, calling" for us to partake of his body and to drink from his cup.

3/27/94

Washing Another's Feet

John 13:1-17

Momentarily, we will share the bread and the cup of Communion in obedience to the command of Christ. Precisely, the four Gospels reveal that Jesus commands all believers to be baptized as an outward display of our spiritual rebirth and to share, as believers, the bread and the cup of his supper as an outward reminder of the giving of his body and blood for our salvation.

It is of interest to note the sequence of events that occur during what we recall as the last supper. According to Luke "a dispute...arose among [the disciples] as to which one of them was to be regarded as the greatest" in the kingdom of God (22:24).

While the conversation was going on among the disciples, Jesus got up and began to enact one of the significant dramatic scenes of the ages: washing the feet of the disciples (vv. 2, 4–5).

It was Albert Schweitzer who said, "I don't know what your destiny will be, but one thing I do know: the only ones among you who will be happy are those who will have sought and found how to serve."

One insight we might gather from this morning's meditation is the will amid our conversations and interactions with one another to look away and behold what Jesus is up to. As Jesus began his tour of feet-washing, the buzz of conversation among the disciples no doubt became as quiet as the moments before dawn.

Mouths that had been unhinged seeking to be heard became locked. Eyes that had rotated from one voice to another became focused upon the kneeling posture of Jesus and the ministrations of his wet hands.

And as he knelt before each of them, the water's chill from the bathing cloth sent a breath-taking message to healed hearts, while the tender touch, gloved in the drying cloth, brought moist tears to disciplined eyes.

When the presence of Jesus and his subservient nature interrupts our careless, self-centered, egotistic pride, our hearts are wounded and our identity is speared.

After washing their feet, he dried his hands, rejoining the still quiet, speechless group—and said with words what he had done with his hands (vv. 12–17).

Therefore, in the midst of our quarrels, let us look aside to see what Jesus is up to. In our pride let us look aside to see what Jesus is up to.

In our doubt let us look aside to see what Jesus is up to. In our despair let us look aside to see what Jesus is up to.

While his disciples were embroiled in "who's number one?," Jesus knelt among them to be the least.

While we quarrel to assert our rights, Jesus kneels among us, faithful to duty.

While we list all of our accomplishments to verify our fame, Jesus kneels among us to lift the cross upon his shoulders.

While we doubt that anyone cares for us, Jesus kneels in front of us to rinse our feet.

While we flounder in despair, wandering for direction in life, Jesus prepares the basin and doffs his robe. And Jesus speaks to us, saying, "You are blessed if you do likewise" (v. 17).

So as we move to his table, let our bantering cease because our eyes have beheld the humility of our Lord and our ears have heard the gracious benediction acclaiming service. Our dry mouths will accept the bread as of his body; our lips will sip the flow as of his blood; and we should never, ever be the same again.

3/1/92

The Best Is Yet To Be

John 2:1-11

While we would classify the changing of water into wine as a miracle, in John's Gospel the writer calls it a sign—the first sign of Jesus—for it revealed his glory. Disciples Peter, Andrew, Philip, and Nathanael were witnesses to the miracle, as we call it, and no doubt enjoyed the wine.

However, the writer designated their response as, "Having seen his glory revealed...his disciples believed in him" (v. 11).

It is as though in this remarkable event that transpired in a most simple, unostentatious, and unheralded manner, the disciples realized it was he with whom they were to be linked from that moment into eternity. The majestic glory of God almighty is not beyond us or behind us but is poured out into our real world.

The glory of God's Son is revealed to one's faith that discerns the sign and the direction in which it points. We are prone to see and stand transfixed. Yet the person of faith, in awe, sees and perceives what is yet to be.

The direction is not marked by profound philosophical twists, secret codes, or by learning fraternal handshakes for inclusion. Rather, in this case, it is learned by a plain, popular joke. The mystery of the availing mastery of Jesus in our lives is not found in lofty dreams, but in actual situations in which we find ourselves from one moment to the next.

And the joke?

"Everyone serves the good wine first, and then the inferior wine after the guests have drunk freely. But you have kept the good wine until now" (v. 10).

The steward of the festivities tells this innocent joke, and the Gospel writer transposes this whispered joke into a remarkable parable. When Jesus is present in our lives, the best is yet to be.

That is the way Jesus ever deals with his people, revealing his glory and calling forth their faith.

Momentarily, we will taste the wafer and sip the juice. It will not be rated five stars in taste, according to its goodness. However, we will be mindful that as Jesus presents himself among us, we behold his glory, and our faith is compelled—for the best is yet to be.

10/6/96

Stretch Out Your Hand

John 6:35, 51b, 54

Momentarily, bread will be distributed in the room to the believing community. Each of us will extend our hands to receive the bread as an act of faith.

Faith is an outstretched hand, and it is love that fills the hand. Remember, in Mark's Gospel (3:5), Jesus said to the man with a withered hand, "Stretch out your hand!"

Following the eating of the bread, the cup will be shared in individual containers. Each of us will extend our hands to receive our portion of the cup as an act of faith.

Faith is an outstretched hand, and it is love that fills the hand. By extending your hand of faith to receive and to eat the bread and to receive and to drink the cup, do you realize that you are in a minority?

Many who had heard Jesus speak and had been witness to his miracles found a reason to turn away and no longer follow him.

We are at a disadvantage to really understand—because we know the whole story and have heard it over and over again. However, let's "play like" we are among his original audience and that his words are new to our hearing: "I am the bread of life. Whoever comes to me will never be hungry, and whoever believes in me will never be thirsty" (v. 35); "and the bread I will give for the life of the world is my flesh...unless you eat my flesh and drink my blood, you have no life in you...for my flesh is true food and my blood is true drink" (vv. 51b, 53b-54).

Do these words offend us? No. Why? Because Jesus was not speaking literally—for he said, "The words that I have spoken to you are spirit and life" (6:63b).

In our faith tradition we interpret his words symbolically; the bread symbolizes his body given for us, and the cup symbolizes his blood shed for us.

However, it is understandable that those who first heard these words might have responded, "This teaching is too difficult for us" (6:60). And as a result they turned away from Jesus, going separate paths.

It requires indomitable faith, at times to the point of appearing to be ridiculous, to publicly extend our hands into the hands of God. Yet for those who do, withered hands are healed, empty vessels are filled, and lost hope is engendered.

As many chose to turn away from Jesus, he asked his disciples, "Do you wish also to go away?" (6:67). Peter responded for them, saying, "Lord, to whom can we go? You have the words of eternal life. We have come to believe and to know that you are the Holy One of God" (6:68-69).

Many with physical sight and hearing did not see and hear Jesus for who he was. Indeed, it was difficult. They were blind to the evidence of the spirit and deaf to the stirring of the wind.

But a few did see the seeable and hear the movement of the wind. They were not offended by the grotesqueness of the imagery. They stretched forth their hands, in faith, to receive both the flesh of God's incarnation and the blood of redemption.

Therefore, with your own eyes this morning see the bread, see his flesh, his body broken for you. And with your own ears listen for the flow of blood; listen and hear that "without the shedding of blood there is no forgiveness of sin" (Heb. 9:22b).

6/7/98

Being One With Others

John 10:16

Today we are to be involved in fulfilling the fundamental order of the Lord: "Do this in remembrance of me." We are to do what he did with the words he himself spoke when he gave his body and his blood in the form of the bread and the wine to his disciples as a pledge of eternal life.

Therefore, what is to happen momentarily is an event not of the past, but our very own happening in this place, at this time, within the now presence of the Lord. We are always the many for whom One died. We are those who have been redeemed. Our salvation rests upon the event of Jesus—his life, death, and resurrection.

Yet the reality of our salvation is much more than an event wedged between the eons before Christ and the twenty centuries since. So when we meet at his table, we are not reenacting an incident from the scattered past. Christ is both remembered and present.

His life, death, and resurrection—events of the past—are realities within the symbolism of the Lord's Supper, which now become realities of our much-needed present encounters. For it is not only that we meet to simply remember Christ but that we also meet to be met by him today. I proclaim, then, that Christ is present with us today.

He is present as the gift of eternal life. He is present as the unity of love among us. He is present as the friend of the friendless. He is present as the fellow traveler of the wanderer. He is present as the brother of the child of God.

All that we cannot be, Christ is present to give. He gives us life rather than death. The one and only demand of us is an active faith in the presence today of what the Lord accomplished for us.

As we look toward his table, we see the bread and cup—not of the past, but of the present. We meet the Lord—not of the past, but ever present. We never meet at his table in the past, but always in the present.

The Lord gives himself today to nourish our bodies, to strengthen us for this day, and to ensure our steadfastness. The Word became flesh and dwells among us. Let us therefore go and see what the Lord has made unto us—now!

10/4/98

Three Acts

Matthew 4:19; 1 Corinthians 11:24; Acts 3:6

Act One: Jesus said, "Follow me" (Matt. 4:19). To ordinary people this extraordinary man invited them into a unique fellowship, encouraging them to imitate him: "Follow me!"

Act Two: Jesus said, "Do this in memory of me" (1 Cor. 11:24). To ordinary people this extraordinary man invited them to an unusual supper at the conclusion of which he broke bread and shared a cup and pled with them, "Remember me!"

Act Three: Soon after Jesus was gone, two men who had "followed" him gave witness that they would "remember" him. So they said to a forty-year-old lame man, "Rise and walk!" (Acts 3:6). To follow Christ is to give extraordinary witness to having had fellowship with him.

The Conclusion: The essence of the Christian faith is ordinary people doing extraordinary things in remembrance of Christ.

7/22/90

Sermons for Holy Week and Easter

"God turned the evil deed of Good Friday into the glorious dawn of Easter. Easter is the rainbow after the storm. And I, nor my world, nor you, will ever be the same."

—Jon Appleton, 1986

"It Is Finished"

Psalm 22:27-31; John 19:28-30

Almost every day we talk about finishing things. There is a welcomed sigh when the kitchen is cleaned or when winter clothes have been stored away. There is a sense of pride when the car is washed or when the carpet is vacuumed.

There is a good feeling when we staple the sheets of a term paper or when we send our completed tax forms to the IRS. There is a sense of pride upon making the final payment on a car note. There is a good, good feeling when the clock is punched on Friday afternoon.

We delight in finishing things. However, do we really ever finish doing things?

A clean kitchen after an evening meal has the odor of bacon grease and the litter of coffee grounds and egg-stained dishes the next morning. A cleaned and polished car of the morning is streaked with pollen by evening. One term paper finished awaits the next assignment. And do we ever finalize all our debts?

Oh, we finish some things, like the twelfth grade—and even receive a certificate of graduation—while actually never finally finishing much of anything.

But the sixth word of Jesus from the cross is, "It is finished!" Within himself Jesus had done all that he could do.

But what is the antecedent of the pronoun *it*? Some would say his earthly life and ministry; others, perhaps, his purpose upon earth. Others call it "the Great Bridge." In a sense none of these is untrue. However, there is another antecedent that stands taller than all the previously mentioned ones. That is "the cup." "The cup is finished!"

Some six weeks before the cross, the mother of James and John had asked Jesus if her two sons might be acclaimed the first in his kingdom, one on his right hand and the other on his left. Jesus replied (looking at the disciples), "Are you able to drink of the cup which I am on the verge of drinking?"

A few hours before, in Gethsemane, Jesus had pled, "Father, if it is possible, let this cup pass from me." Now, on the cross, he shouts, "It is finished!"

Symbolically, he lifts up an empty cup. However, his is not a despairing shout. He got rid of his doubts in Gethsemane.

His is a shout of triumph: My Father's will is my will. His will is that all might have life. The empty cup puts him squarely in the will of God. The empty cup puts him squarely in our place, the place of death.

"God was in Christ, reconciling the world unto himself" (2 Cor. 5:19).

The cumulative forces of evil had prevailed—nailing Jesus to the cross. But that deathly deed was outreached by God's reconciling love—that could stretch deeper than our lives are low. His mission revealed that love works its way under, to lift and to restore.

Romans 6:23 tells us, "The wages of sin is death, but the gift of God is eternal life through Jesus Christ our Lord." But why the cross?

Jesus had fed the hungry—but did not finish the pangs of hunger. He had healed the sick—but even the Great Physician did not finish the prevalence of disease and affliction. He had taught with authority—but did not finish the doubts of many scoffers.

However, there was one thing he could finish—and that was "the cup." By drinking it as an act of the will of God, not even the will of evil (death), which had nailed him to the cross, could prevail against him. A continuing string drawn through the pages of the Bible reaches its foremost revelation in this shout of triumph from the cross.

Joseph had said it to his brothers, centuries before, in Egypt: "What you meant for evil, God has turned into good" (Genesis 45). No matter the dastardly blows we suffer, nothing can pull us away from the love of God.

Jesus had said, "When lifted up from the earth, I will draw everyone to myself" (John 12:32). Spiritual magnetism—he had it.

When these words were spoken, however, they fell on deaf ears. But when he was "lifted up," the denying Peter was transformed into a powerful, Spirit-filled preacher. Jesus' words "It is finished!" gave rhyme to poets, heart to martyrs, courage to the faint, hope to the lost, and belief to the scoffers.

When James and John were asked if they could drink from the cup, they replied, "We are able." And do you recall the response of Jesus? It was, "You will indeed" (Matt. 20:23).

Today, the cup is placed in our hands. And because Jesus finished for us death's sting, we are enabled by his Spirit to be finished with despair, to learn from losses, to withstand defeats, to work through hate, to counter betrayals, and to even accept death itself.

Jesus is the "author and finisher" of our faith. What we cannot finish for ourselves, Jesus finishes for us, triumphantly.

4/09/95

To See Jesus

John 12:20-32

Often on Sunday mornings when I first came to Athens, Duella Wynn would come to my study before going to teach the M&M class. She came with positive words to encourage me.

It was not unusual for her to bring a gift: a book from her husband's library, a poem, or a flower. One Sunday she brought me this brass strip, set in a triangular stand, with the inscription, "Sir, we would see Jesus."

As the years have come and gone in preparations for sermons, my eyes have often rested on Mrs. Wynn's gift, and I have recalled her words as she gave it to me: "This is why we gather to worship each Sunday—to see Jesus."

Living in a world with so much to see and with so many options vying for our attention, time is still taken to gather in worship—so we may "see Jesus."

All who lead in worship and teaching are in the position of Philip when the Greeks approached him, saying, "Sir, we would see Jesus."

Why is seeing so significant? Well, to see is to know. To see is to believe. To see is a term that means "to experience." Experiential knowledge does not just inform us; it also transforms us.

To see is to lift up, to rightly perceive, to behold a demonstration. When the Greeks saw Jesus, they heard him proclaim that he would be "lifted up" so he might "draw people" to himself (John 12:32).

The story of salvation is not finished until Christ is "lifted up" by us in what we proclaim and in how we live. Paul told the Galatians: "It is no longer I who live, but it is Christ who lives through me" (2:20).

In seeing Christ a fire begins to burn within us. Jeremiah spoke to Israel as though his tongue were aflame, speaking for God, "I will put my law within them, and I will write it upon their hearts; and I will be their God, and they shall be my people" (31:33).

From Moses at the burning bush to the Pentecostal tongues of fire, fire is a symbol of the incandescent presence of God. Hebrews 12:29 affirms, "Our God is a consuming fire." God's covenant, grace, and presence through Christ sear and seal our hearts.

The Greeks came to see Jesus, not some reflection of their own lives. We gather in worship to see Jesus, not some reflection of our own lives. We want our hearts to burn within us. Seeing Jesus changes the way we see everything and everybody.

Two disciples, returning to Emmaus after the crucifixion, were joined by a third man. They did not recognize him to be Jesus until they saw him break bread for them. To one another they said, "Were not our hearts burning within us while he was opening the scriptures to us?" (Luke 24:32).

The reality of new birth is to have our hearts aflame, our vision focused, our imagination released, and our sight enlarged. It is within our ability to see that power is released in our lives. To not see is to be imprisoned; to see is to be empowered. Spirituality is the art of spiritually seeing—first seeing things as they are and then seeing in those things what might become. To see Jesus empowers us to look beyond the scope of our own desires. As we experience the transforming power of Jesus, we see him bending to the needs of people, begetting hope in the distraught, touching lepers, lifting children, and comforting women of ill repute and men of ill temperament.

Upon seeing Jesus we see ourselves—and his will to empower us to relinquish our control that leads us down blind alleys. It is under his control that we find the way to eternal living.

A seminary graduate, upon receiving his appointment from the bishop, quickly became distraught—and started grousing, grumbling, and complaining because he felt his assignment was less than he deserved. A friend who loved him dearly but was unsympathetic to his griping patted him on the back and said, "Bill, you know the world is a better place because Michelangelo didn't say, 'I don't do ceilings.'"

The world is a better place because:
Moses didn't say, "I don't do rivers."
Or Noah didn't say, "I don't do arks."
Or Jeremiah didn't say, "I don't do weeping."
Or David didn't say, "I don't do giants."
Or Peter didn't say, "I don't do Gentiles."
Or Mary Magdalene didn't say, "I don't do feet."
Or Paul didn't say, "I don't do letters."
Or, most importantly, Jesus didn't say, "I don't do crosses."

"Sir, we would see Jesus." May that be our desire—to be ready to do whatever Jesus desires, even those things we ordinarily may not want to do.

3/20/94

Good Friday: To Despair

Matthew 27:45-46

For the longest little while one Friday, God walked out on his only Son. If we ever think sin is not serious business, we must recall the loud shout, *Eli, Eli, lema sabachthani?* "My God! My God! Why did you abandon me?"

This shout of doubt becomes for us words of loving identity—perhaps the most human words found in all of history.

If we ever think Jesus is not serious business, we must recall the loud shout, "My God! My God! Why did you abandon me?"

His cross, and those three hours of darkness, ripped the page of eternity. That which is eternal—time—stopped. That which is space was reversed.

The moon can be eclipsed, but not the sun. Oh, it can be clouded and somewhat covered, but never totally eclipsed. Yet it was; there was darkness from noon to the third hour.

This was, at that time, the most abnormal moment of all times—and abides as history's number-two day, depicting the awfulness and the depravity of humanity. History's number-one day is Easter Sunday, which depicts the grace, glory, and love of God and his Son—but we must wait to celebrate that glorious day.

If we ever think God is not serious about sin, never forget that in those hours of the cross, not only did darkness fall upon the earth, but it extinguished the Light of the World. Even God the Father could not face what his Son suffered. Sensing the absence of God creates a ghastly hole.

T. S. Eliot wrote, "You do not know what hope is until you have lost it. You only know what it is not to hope. You do not know what it is to have hope taken from you."

We have our examples of this truth: We lose a parent or a spouse or a child or a friend. In time most of us lose something dear—and if we were to lose God, what then?

Jesus, the Light of the World, was overcome by darkness for three eerie, agonizing hours. Faith's road is rough, and the Bible makes no bones about it. We must look today more closely at the cross. Who was this man?

His first three words of love identify Jesus as God and as man:

"Father, forgive them" (Jesus offers loving forgiveness).

"Today, you will be with me" (Jesus offers loving assurance).

"Woman behold...son behold" (Jesus offers loving comfort).

This fourth word of loving identity, however, places Jesus squarely with you and me. He does not bottle up his despair nor whistle in the dark. He does not point to a passing star. He does not hide his humiliation, but shouts the loudest, most human cry of universal identity: "My God! My God! Why? Why me?"

The alpha of this cry collided with the omega of accepting the cup in Gethsemane. Even God's Son upon this earth did not pass himself off as having arrived completely immune to unhappiness and faithlessness.

Jesus is saying, "I am whipped!" "I am defenseless!" It takes courage to disbelieve. Thank God for this shout of doubt! For in so doing, Jesus boldly identifies with each of us.

He was not a machine made by God to mock our mortality. In this hour of dying, Jesus was only human, but in a most and mighty divine way.

At that time when God walked out, Jesus went back to a place where God had been seen (Psalm 22). When the water gets muddy, give it time to clear up. When it is dark, await the sunrise.

A godly person may throw up his or her hands in despair, but if done in prayer and not bitterness, he or she will soon find God again.

It is not unusual for us to lose faith; after all, we are only human and have a way of losing many things. When we lose our car keys, we decry the loss, then desperately attempt to reconstruct when and where we had them last. So it is when we lose touch with God—and so it was with his Son.

The faith of our fathers (and mothers) may snap for us under too much pressure, especially if we have borrowed their faith and have not experienced our own. But our fathers' and mothers' God does not snap. In the midst of Calvary's despair, Jesus still called to God out of hope's habit.

In the valley our faith may die—but not God. In the extremity of suffering on the cross, the cry of Jesus was "My God! My God!" Searching for identity, Jesus simply needed to feel God's hand.

God will not leave us even though we are lost in our despair. This is the "good news"—God will not leave us even if our faith runs out.

The lost despair of our Lord begins on the note, "My God! My God! Why?"—but there was a triumphant ending to Psalm 22: "People not yet born will be told, 'The LORD saved his people.'"

We may doubt our faith, yet God will not leave us.

3/15/98

The Resurrection Conspiracy

John 20:19-22

A number of years ago a book titled *The Passover Plot* claimed that the resurrection story and most of the recorded, subsequent events were really acts of a conspiracy conducted by the followers of Jesus to perpetuate his name and magnify their own status.

The word *conspiracy* has sinister implications for us. Hearing the term, we think of spy rings, espionage, cloaks, and exploits. Robert Ludlum has made his mark as a master in contriving deep-rooted conspiracies. But I would like for you to hear what E. B. White wrote about conspiracy from a totally different context. Following the death of his wife he wrote, "Katherine was a member of the resurrection conspiracy, the company of those who plant seeds of hope under dark clouds of grief or oppression, going about their living and dying until no one knows how, when, or where the tender Easter shoots appear, and a piece of creation is healed."

Actually, the word *conspiracy* is an exact description of what really did happen when Jesus commissioned his disciples, the evening of his resurrection day. John says that Jesus "breathed on them." *Spiro* is Latin for "breathing." The word *conspiro* originally meant a group of people so closely bound that they literally breathed together.

So in that house, with all the doors locked, it was the breath of Jesus upon his disciples that indeed created a "resurrection conspiracy." It was much later that the word *conspiracy* became restricted in its meaning to designate individuals or groups of sinister characters who were up to no good.

In a world full of conspirators—plotting to overthrow governments, terrorize populations, cheat unwary investors, spread misinformation—isn't it refreshing to leap back into history and discover a conspiracy ignited by the breath of Jesus, that if never snuffed out will lead people to light and to new life?

Jesus said, "Just as my Father has sent me forth, so I am now sending you" (v. 21). Matthew gives the same report regarding Jesus' commandment at ascension: "Go then and make disciples of all the nations, baptizing them into the name of the Father, the Son, and the Holy Spirit, teaching them to practice all the commands I have given you. And I will be with you always, to the end of the age" (28:19–20).

Jesus breathed into them and sent them into a hostile world. In our day the church is out in the open; steeples are a part of our landscape, and religious celebrations often coincide with worldly holidays.

It is difficult for us to appreciate the limitations and terror in the early years of the church. Christians were accused of sinister activity. They were tried and suffered as martyrs, as members of a heretical sect, as subversives plotting to undermine Rome, and as practitioners of immorality (cannibalism). Yet they continued to witness to the resurrection, a conspiracy of love and hope and healing, amid a society bent on subjection, cruelty, and control.

In a time when life was cheap, these conspirators cared for the weak and helpless. In a time when fear lay as a cloud over anxious people, these conspirators demonstrated a love that would cast out fear. In a time when death was viewed as the final terror, these conspirators spoke confidently of resurrection and were heard singing as they were led into flames of martyrdom.

A Roman observer noted, "If any righteous man among the Christians passes from the world, they rejoice and offer thanks to God, and they escort his body with songs and thanksgiving, as if he were setting out from one place to another nearby."

That was the early church in the hostile world, to which Christ had sent them. Breathed upon by Jesus, they prevailed in the world because they conspired with his promised presence to overcome that world.

The world we live in (the world to which Christ sends us) is crammed with negative forces: death-dealing conspiracies, voices that flaunt unsecured promises, and advertisements that offer so much for so little. Yet the same Christ breathes upon us—today's disciples—enlisting and empowering us to work as conspirators in a hostile environment.

Champions of renown come to mind, like Mother Teresa, working quietly and selflessly amid the wretched conditions in the slums of Calcutta; and Lynda Bethea, a Baptist missionary to Kenya who was killed recently when she and her husband, Ralph, stopped to assist what appeared to be someone hurt and sprawled across a rural Kenyan road. They were less than a mile from their intended destination when this forty-two-year-old mother of four died.

There are millions of unnamed, "breath-filled" followers of Jesus whose stories are not publicly known but who conspire daily to confront life's infernal forces. They bring hope to despair, food to hunger, joy to sorrow, peace to terror, healing to the diseased, and life to death.

I see these people every day of my life: a tending wife at the bedside of her husband, daughters gathered around their mother, neighbors mowing another's lawn. When tragedy erupts, there is soon food bulging in a refrigerator, clothes piled in sizes, and linens stacked high on a makeshift cot in response to a burned-out home. And in more normal times there is a father throwing batting practice to his son and mothers waiting in lined cars for ballet practice to end; people sending letters of cheer and hope to military personnel they may not know, yet writing in the name of Christ.

The breath of Jesus still fills the lungs of those who see him clearly and who take his call seriously. The resurrection conspiracy is not dead. It is at work, like leaven in the lump, and its work is most effectively traversed with both mighty and weak hands.

Sometimes we need to move mountains and other times the expertise to blend ingredients in precise measure to bake a cake or cook a casserole. We witness the conspiracy at work every week of our lives.

It was not the presentation of a religious institution that Jesus had in a mind when he said, "As the Father sent me, so I send you!" But rather he breathed into living people a new life force to convey his kingdom of love for which he gave his life from one person to another person.

Remember Gideon? He was called by God from the humblest position in his father's house. Remember Moses? He was called by God from a burning bush. Like him, we too are inclined to ask, "Who? Me?"

Likewise, we wonder, how can I have any real impact where I live and work on the course of events in this hostile world? I have little spiritual power, limited biblical knowledge, and no ability to speak.

The returning answer, however, is that it is not our breath that propels us. It is not into a religious club that we have been baptized, but a community that has been breathed upon by Christ.

The breath of Christ is within us, uniting us and urging us in a conspiracy of love and life eternal. We are conspirators of Christ, those "who plant seeds of hope under dark clouds," confident that, in given time, "tender Easter shoots will appear, and a piece of creation will be healed."

4/7/91

Resurrections: His and Ours

John 20:1-18

Management guru Peter Drucker suggests that we ought to be able to express our mission statement on a t-shirt. Of course, we live in a village of t-shirted evangelists: "I shop; therefore, I am"; "Life is golf. Everything else is details."

Paul had a mission statement: "I'm pressing on!" So did Peter: "I'm following on!" And Andrew: "I'm bringing others to Jesus!"

What would be Jesus' mission statement? "I am the way, the truth, and the life!" This one says it all: "I am the resurrection!"

Jesus was not born with a silver spoon in his mouth. People raised eyebrows about his birth. His unmarried mother went out of town to have her baby, then lived for quite a while in Egypt before returning home to Nazareth. His ancestral lineage was significant, but his father was a peasant carpenter with limited status and standing.

Jesus was a Jew—a member of a despised racial and religious minority. He was a citizen of an occupied country, a people looked down upon by the Romans and despised by neighboring nations.

He was heir to a religious tradition known for its puritanical legalism and precise judgmentalism that functioned best in isolation and delighted in prescribing an outer court for women sinners and Gentiles. With such a confining and judicial background, Jesus could have been oversensitive, reactionary, or defensive.

However, he never joined a guerrilla band in the mountains nor led a demonstration against Rome. His education was limited; he was untraveled, and it was said of him that he attracted losers. The records revealed that he died a pauper.

His path of faith rose to great adulation, only to fall in disarray. He had no home to call his own. He was despised and ridiculed by religious leaders and political authorities. He was betrayed by one of his own disciples, and his other disciples scattered at his arrest. He was denied by one of his closest followers and died on a cross, condemned as a criminal.

He was buried in a borrowed tomb. His identity as a "man of sorrows" seemingly says it all. Yet Jesus is the reason we are here this morning. He is the reason that cathedrals echo his name and clapboard churches laud him with praise and people meet clandestinely to lift him up as King of Kings and Lord of Lords.

Why? Just as eyebrows have always been raised concerning the manner of the birth of Jesus, there have also been questions about the reality of his resurrection. Easter morning's first report to the disciples, according to John's Gospel, was not "He is risen!" but rather Mary Magdalene hysterically shouting, "They have taken the Lord from the tomb, and we don't know where they have put him!" (v. 2).

With our advantage of knowing the whole story, we are prone to question their confusion and anxiety. He had given testimony, by deeds and by words, of his resurrection and theirs. All they had to do was look into a mirror to behold the transformation that had been wrought in their own lives. Jesus had resurrected within them meaning out of meaninglessness.

While following in his steps, they had witnessed the blind seeing, the lame walking, and the leper being cleansed. They had heard Jesus resurrect courage with words like "What you sow, you reap"; "What you spend, you will not lose"; "Sit toward the back; be called to the front"; "What you keep, you lose"; "What you give, you receive a hundredfold."

Crisscrossing Galilee, Samaria, and Judea with Jesus, they saw him extend a resurrected power in the lives of seemingly wasted people. A prostitute gained a vision of purity; a tax-collector became a benefactor; a widow beaconed as a scion of generosity; and a Pharisee, by night, received the light of God's redeeming love and the reality of a new birth.

Jesus taught the multitudes using practical parables. He taught his disciples their inner meanings and demanded of them the commandment of love. Where hate seethed, he resurrected love; where darkness prevailed, he resurrected light; where pride presided, he resurrected humility; and where death reigned, he resurrected life.

At daybreak, in the morning hours, at noon, in the afternoon, at dusk, even at midnight, Jesus went about doing resurrections. Granted his impoverishment, his meager and trite physical and material holdings, his path has little to show as we look for things.

Yet in his path of faith, he left many an opened tomb from which people were resurrected to a new life. Bartimaeus, the blind beggar who asked that he might see again, did see again! Behold, the resurrection!

Zacchaeus, the arrogant tax collector, a man of selfish conspiracy, became a man of benevolent generosity. Behold, the resurrection!

The woman at the well, worldly, callous, embittered, lonely, became the one who led her whole village to Jesus. Behold, the resurrection!

Lazarus, buried for four days, lived again. Behold, the resurrection!

The thief, Jesus' neighbor on the cross, the one who in his pain asked Jesus to remember him, was assured in residence in paradise that very day. Behold, the resurrection!

Thus, when Jesus had said to them, "I am the resurrection and life," it was a testimony to what he daily had been doing among them and for them. So on this glorious Easter morning—when resurrection shines upon our own paths of faith—let us not be surprised when hearing Jesus say, "Those who believe in me can overcome all things, even death itself."

The reality of his resurrection long predated his resurrection on Easter morning, as he raised others from their tombs—imparting meaning, courage, power, and love. That resurrection power is reaffirmed in our lives each time "one of the least" of us is raised from our tombs to find meaning amid despair, courage above fear, power in spite of our weakness, and a love that never fails.

Jesus' path of faith left new life in its wake. Our paths of faith inherit his resurrection power. Let us share Paul's mission statement: "I'm pressing on! I can press on through all things through Christ who resurrects me!"

Easter 4/12/98

"I Have Seen the Lord!"

John 20:1, 11-18

"Now on the first day of the week, Mary Magdalene came to the tomb early, while it was still dark" (v. 1). She brought no gifts—neither gold, nor frankincense, nor myrrh—to anoint the body, not even flowers for the grave. She came while it was still dark, when the light that had come into the world had gone out and darkness prevailed.

She came to the tomb early, before anyone else stirred, to see the place where they had laid him. She came to say a word to the dead that she could not utter to anyone living. She came for what we now call "closure."

When hope dies, it must not linger on and on. We must lay death to rest and go on with our lives. We cannot keep going back to the office to see how things are going after the retirement dinner. And though we can return to campus or to the old neighborhood, someone else now lives in our old room or in our old house.

We know from experience that endings are a part of life. It is clear in today's scripture that Mary had not come early to the tomb expecting resurrection, just as we visit not the gravesite of a loved one expecting a literal resurrection.

We are so encumbered by death that it takes time for our eyes and our minds and our faith to catch up. When she found the tomb empty, she was distressed. When one of the angels asked, "Woman, why are you weeping?" her retort was, "They have taken away our Lord, and I do not know where they have laid him."

We sense hopelessness, despondency, and despair in one who had been resolute, trusting, and expectant. Of all the women in the Gospel story, more is said of Mary Magdalene during Jesus' ministry and death than any other. We can imagine her physical exhaustion and emotional trauma having witnessed his crucifixion.

She had been near enough to have touched him when he died, standing next to his mother. It took great gumption for Mary, who had been a Calvary witness and a long Saturday agonizer, to be astir and so resolute to walk among the tombs "while it was still dark."

Why, why was she there so early and alone? Is the question really necessary? Not for those of us who have traveled the valley of death's shadow. Death has humbled us to our knees and robbed us of energy, acceptance, awareness, and candor. Our minds say "yes," but our hearts say "no!"

Death defies our normalcy, energizes our ineptitude, triggers our anger, handcuffs our abilities, and leaves us in its wake, though alive, walking among the tombs, looking for the tomb.

Mark's Gospel tells us that Mary had seen "where the body was laid" (15:47). She had seen the place of Jesus' burial. She had returned to say goodbye, just as we slip back to the gravesites of our beloved. She had not arrived early expecting resurrection. She came to confirm what she knew: Jesus was dead and buried.

Jesus had opened a door for her. Luke's Gospel records that Mary had been cured by Jesus of evil spirits—forces that ruled within her. Jesus had closed the door to her self-serving desire and opened a new door to the "habit" of ministering to the needs of others (8:2-3).

So there she was at the tomb of the one who had opened a new door for her. She returned there to shut it. In him she had become a new creation. Now she knew not what would be. However, she knew he was dead; that reality could not be denied. She could not go on believing. She was there to close the door.

We all know about that, don't we? An airliner falls from the sky, and thirty-five people are consumed in its explosion. On Good Friday I held the hand of a friend whose body is wasting away to cancer's onslaught. I fed a Popsicle to a ten-year-old Monday evening whose gaze was stark and whose little body jerked in seizures. And all of this was happening during Holy Week.

A couple feels the coldness of the closed doors of parenthood. A forty-eight-year-old man is jobless, cold, outside the door of employment. A marriage of twenty-eight years closes down in divorce. We know all about Mary Magdalene's walk among the tombs, seeking the tomb.

But wait a moment. Mary finds the tomb, but the body was not there. Jesus' death could not be verified. Mary had come with her own expectation, with her mind made up, with her comprehension, with her loss, and with her will to close the door. But Jesus was not there.

Note that she did not run to the disciples exclaiming resurrection. Listen to what she did say: "They have taken the Lord out of the tomb, and we do not know where they have laid him" (v. 2b). She had gone to the tomb to say goodbye. But grave robbers had aborted her attempt at closure. In other words, she could not close the door. And the crack in the door was mind-boggling.

We find Mary back near the tomb weeping. People don't weep at resurrection unless overcome by joy. And it was not joy that Mary experienced. So distraught was she that the two angels dressed in white brought neither fear nor ecstasy. They do not faze her. She speaks to them as to orderlies stripping an empty hospital bed: "They have taken away my Lord, and I do not know where they have laid him" (v. 13b).

If the angels responded, she did not hear any more than we hear words at a funeral. She kept weeping—not the wailing lament of a mourner but weeping borne of weariness, frustration, and anger. Weeping, robbed of its final goodbye. Weeping, because Jesus was dead and she was still alive. Though the old demons no longer had hold of her, neither did anything else.

She turned to leave the empty, cold place and, in turning, sensed someone nearby. She came to him as she had with the angels, hiding not her tears and pleading with him, "Sir, if you have carried him away, tell me where you have laid him, and I will take him away" (v. 15b). And then she hears her name: "Mary."

She remembered hearing it before, but that was crazy. It must be the gardener. No, it couldn't be. She had seen them place him in the tomb. They had sealed the tomb—yet she found the tomb opened, and Jesus was absent.

"Rabboni!" Then she lost it. Grabbing at him, seeking to touch, to grasp, to hold, to embrace. Well, what would we have expected? It was not the time to be *blasé*, saying, "Gee, Jesus, you're a sight for sore eyes."

When your son returned from war, you knew how Mary felt; when your wife smiled up at you following open-heart surgery, you knew how Mary felt; when your father moved his toes following a stroke, you knew how Mary felt.

Jesus said, "Do not hold on to me" (v. 17a). Something new is going on, Mary. It transcends birth and death. Mary, old things have passed away; everything is different now. Mary, it is now the time of the Spirit. Time to speak of empty tombs and to see the back of God. Mary, the door is open, not only for you but for everyone.

"Do not hold me, but go tell the others." Mary, go and tell them without any sign of proof other than your word attached to my word. Go and tell them the truth that cannot be verified. Go, Mary, like the Samaritan woman who left her water jar at the well.

Go, Mary; tell the others, "I have seen the Lord!" Go, Mary; it is not up to you to prove it to them. Go, Mary; just open the door a crack.

Easter 4/7/96

A Pastoral Prayer

Thank You, Lord

By Jon Appleton

Thank you, Lord,
For spring cleaning; for the smell of blossoms and the feel of velvet dirt between our fingers.

Thank you, Lord,
For listening to us when all other ears are closed to us; for taking us seriously.

Thank you, Lord,
For food and shelter and clothing; for friends who spend with us the time of day.

Thank you, Lord,
For times we win; for the confidence that builds when we do our best.

Thank you, Lord,
For straight-forward dialogue; for honest, in-depth monologue.

Thank you, Lord,
For extended hands ready to shake; for sensitive ears ready to listen; for gentle fingers ready to soothe; for opened eyes ready to accept.

Thank you, Lord,
For bridges that span possibilities; for tunnels that move mountains; for elevators that extend our height.

Thank you, Lord,
For being there; for the gifts you have given to us; for the opportunity to grow.

After the style of Jesus.

Amen.

3/6/77

Epilogue

Adapted from the funeral meditation for Jon Appleton, November 30, 2016, by Paul A. Baxley, senior minister of the First Baptist Church of Athens, Georgia

A Good Name and Loving Favor

By Paul A. Baxley

A good name is rather to be desired than great riches, and loving favor rather than silver and gold. (Prov. 22:1)

Those words of Proverbs were invoked by Jon Appleton at the beginning of every funeral sermon I ever heard him deliver, so I cannot stand here today without reciting them myself. And I cannot help but notice how incredibly true they became for him.

By our presence we bear witness to the abiding goodness of Jon's name in this church, in this community, and far beyond. Moreover, we carry in our hearts an undeniable loving favor for him.

Almost all of us knew Jon first and most as pastor. He was a pastor to this congregation officially for twenty-three years, and he carried a pastoral identity for many of us in this church long after he retired.

He stood with so many in the waters of baptism, preached from this pulpit, presided at the Lord's table, stood with 450 couples at marriage altars, kept watch with many in hospital rooms, and walked with us in this church and community through life's darkest valleys, officiating at about 750 funerals. He loved the church; he loved this church and its people, and we carry the influence of that love in our hearts with loving favor.

Jon's pastoral identity extended far beyond this congregation. People throughout this community saw Jon as a pastor, and there are Baptist ministers in this state and far beyond who not only knew Jon as a pastoral colleague, but also as a mentor and tremendous pastoral influence. I dare say that for almost all of us, the name Jon Appleton is profoundly connected to his identity as a pastor.

For that reason a reading from Ephesians 4:11-13 is profoundly appropriate. Paul told the Ephesians that God gave some people gifts to be pastors, just as God gifted others for other roles in the life of the church. There is no doubt that God gave Jon tremendous pastoral gifts.

God gifted Jon for pastoral ministry through a father who modeled the pastoral life for him and who throughout Jon's life was his most significant example of pastoral ministry. Even when I met Jon long after his retirement, he was still speaking of the powerful influence of his father in his ministry and his faith. That was a gift.

God gifted Jon for pastoral ministry through the gift of Virginia, who became a full partner in Christian ministry. From the time they met at Ridgecrest Baptist Conference Center in North Carolina six decades ago, throughout their married life, Virginia was an amazing gift to Jon! Virginia gave herself to Jon, not only encouraging his ministry but participating fully in the life of the church and its people.

I cannot tell you how many people have shared stories with me of the ways Virginia invited them to this church or called them if they missed the Sunday school class she and Jon started after arriving here. The love Virginia and Jon shared was an inspiration and example for so many.

Virginia, your ability to be fully engaged in church while also using your gifts in your own work allowed you to set an example for succeeding generations of ministerial families. There is no doubt that just as Jon's father was a gift for his ministry, so were you.

God gifted Jon for pastoral ministry by giving him a remarkable relational charisma. That charisma enabled him to invite new people into the congregation while also building and maintaining relationships of love and trust and providing care in the most difficult seasons of life.

So many people could bear witness to the ways Jon walked with them through dark valleys and difficult seasons, observing carefully, listening compassionately, offering steadfast presence, and embodying love. Jon's ability to find the right words at a funeral was one of his most cherished pastoral graces, but his ability to do this was not isolated. I am convinced it was deeply rooted in his relationships with the people whose lives he touched.

God gifted Jon for pastoral ministry by entrusting to him a set of deep theological convictions that were consistently expressed in his distinctly poetic preaching and also profoundly influential for the way he led. A defining theme of Jon's preaching, as reported by church historian Ernie Hynds, was God's mercy symbolized in arms being outstretched to the people.

"Christ seeks and accepts us as we are, not to impose on us to become other than what we are," Jon said. "So much of religion wants to create the carbon-copy type of believer. [Yet] in the disciples you can see the wide difference of personalities that Jesus called."

A sermon preached in June 1991 sets forth Jon's deep convictions about core Baptist tenets and his commitments to them. There and then he held up experiential religion, voluntary participation, spiritual democracy, and inquiring minds as essential for Baptist faith. He summarized his view with these words: "We are a people who have experienced religion voluntarily, and we have chosen to profess this in a congregational, democratic setting with open, inquiring thoughts."

On the last point he declared: "The Baptist minds claimed that no idea was too sacred, no doctrine too rooted, no practice so undeniable to be examined in light of Scripture and the leading of the Holy Spirit. Our heritage is one in which we are not afraid to inquire, to ask, to question, to search Scripture—not for the sake of being obstinate, but in search of truth."

Jon was gifted by God for pastoral ministry not only with a deep set of convictions but even more with a lifelong love of learning. His convictions were nourished and enriched because he gave his life to searching.

He loved to read; his meticulous records indicate that he read 1,700 books and often selected ones that would challenge his point of view. Until very late in life, he continued to read new things and seek conversation partners with whom he could discuss his reading. He did not live his entire ministry out of his young adult faith or his seminary experiences, but rather he continued to ask, seek, and knock—not only to believe in open-mindedness but to practice and model it.

One of the most important gifts God gave Jon for his pastoral ministry was his sharp wit, his incredible sense of humor. Several of Jon's former staff members (who shall be nameless) remember being away on a staff retreat. The ministerial staff had gone out to dinner and was returning to the conference center. Jon was driving the others in the car. He pulled up to the door of the facility, and as he let them out before parking the car, he announced, "Charles Stanley wouldn't do this for you, boys!"

Jon didn't mind telling a funny story about himself or being on the receiving end of a funny exchange. Many of you know about Jon's experience teaching Bible study on a Wednesday night very early in his ministry here. He became distracted while teaching by longtime member, Amoretta Smith, who was scrambling around on the front row looking in her purse for something. So he stopped his lesson to inquire: "Amoretta, what are you looking for?" The congregation exploded in laughter as she replied, "A NoDoz tablet!"

Reflecting on experiences like this early in his ministry, Jon told Ernie Hynds, "It took only three weeks, but I was home."

Sometimes Jon was asked how he stayed at First Baptist Athens so long. His response: "I stayed so long because I knew too many secrets about church members." (You will be glad to know that the family has entrusted that treasure trove of secrets to me for safekeeping.)

Paul told the Ephesians that God gifted some to be pastors, and we know today that God gifted Jon for ministry. Paul also told the Ephesians that pastors were to use their gifts to build up the church.

God used Jon's gift of poetry and theological substance to build the church by preaching sermons that nourished faith, cultivated awareness of mystery, and encouraged open searching.

God used Jon's leadership gifts to build this church physically, as the campus was dramatically renovated and expanded during his tenure.

God used Jon's relational gifts to build this church by inviting a new generation of people into its life and ministry.

God used those same gifts of leadership and relationship to build this church by guiding it through very difficult seasons in Southern Baptist life and helping it remain committed to a historical vision of Baptist identity while remaining united at the same time.

God also used Jon's gifts to build up the larger church. He was deeply invested in building relationships with other clergy in Athens and encouraging cooperation between churches in downtown Athens. He spoke at length with me about how important this was to him.

God also used Jon to build the larger church by being a pastor to those in this community who had no church home. Just as Jon believed Christ's arms open wide in love, so his pastoral energy reached beyond his congregation.

God used Jon to build the church by fostering friendships with other Baptist pastors in and beyond this community, being a valued friend to some and an indispensable mentor to others.

God used Jon to build the church by playing a critical role in creating a new Baptist community in this state and beyond, as he was essential to the establishment of the Cooperative Baptist Fellowship, the Cooperative Baptist Fellowship of Georgia, and McAfee School of Theology.

There is no doubt that God used Jon's tremendous gifts to build the church and that because of Jon's faithfulness many of us in this room are still learning, still seeking, still asking, still growing in our faith. His influence is still profoundly felt here. Even this Sunday, I will baptize a young man who was named Jon, spelled correctly (J-O-N), as a reflection of Jon Appleton's profound influence on his parents.

When we hear the name Jon Appleton, most of us equate his good name with his remarkable and faithful pastoral life. That is understandable. But we must remember that Jon's name meant more than pastor.

Jon was a faithful and loving husband and father, and the members of his family celebrate his life and grieve his death in much more personal ways. One who was for so many of us a pastor, guide, and friend was also a husband to Virginia, a father to Catherine, a father-in-law to Jack, an uncle to Jon, a brother-in-law to Carolyn.

Virginia, there is no doubt that Jon loved you tremendously, that you were light and joy and the love of his life. Catherine, we know that you and your father had an extremely close bond, that you cherish the time you spent with him, the conversations you shared with him—and the lifelong knowledge that the man you saw faithfully preaching and leading a congregation was the daddy to whom you could go home, know, and love. For Jon, being husband and father was a lifelong call and privilege. And we know he also loved and treasured other members of his family.

At his core Jon Appleton was a committed Christian. His deep, personal, experienced faith was expressed in his preaching and teaching, evidenced in his care, seen in his family life, and was present even in the struggles of his final years. As illness weakened him in so many ways, his faithfulness continued.

Those who visited him toward the end experienced something I also experienced. He would grab hold of our hands, hold us tight, for an instant seemingly unwilling to let us go. His love and devotion were that strong. And on one occasion as he held tight, he led church members in prayer.

It wasn't lost on us that Jon died at peace, with eyes open toward heaven, early in the morning on the first Sunday in Advent, just hours before we would light the candle of hope and pray for God's deliverance. In a mystery too profound to be captured by words or reduced to clichés, Jon's final Advent prayer was answered: Emmanuel came to him!

In the words of Jon's beloved Gospel of John, Jesus took Jon to himself so that where he is, Jon will be also forever—loved, kept, held in a house not made with hands, eternal in the heavens, until that day when, by God's marvelous, mysterious grace, we will meet again.

Thanks be to God for the remarkable life and ministry of Jon Appleton. Amen.

Benediction

"May the Father have the joy of your love, his Son the peace of your presence, and the Spirit the assurance of your hope. Amen."
—Jon Appleton, Christmas Day 1988

"Jon Appleton was first and foremost a pastor who loved the church and preached the gospel with clear-eyed conviction…. In the sermons and prayers he meticulously prepared across the years, his insight into what it means to live out the gospel in our times and the inclination of his heart and spirit in worship live on. Dip into this treasury of inspiration, and you will find that Jon's voice still rings true, lifting, instructing, and challenging us."

R. Alan Culpepper,
Dean and Professor Emeritus,
McAfee School of Theology, Mercer University

"For five years I was Jon's associate pastor at First Baptist Athens, Georgia. Jon became a mentor who taught by example. He showed me how to shepherd and love people. He was a true pastor."

Scott Walker,
Director of The Institute of Life Purpose,
Mercer University, Macon, Georgia

"Dr. Appleton reveled in riddles, which he spun frequently to confounded listeners. But when it came to matters of faith, his message was clear: anchor your faith in a journey of thinking, using the brain and soul in which God gifted you, for salvation is a personal and treasured revelation that lasts a lifetime."

Paula Hooper,
Member and colleague,
First Baptist Church, Athens, Georgia

"Margaret and I met Jon and Virginia Appleton at the elevator on the tenth floor of the Galt House in Louisville, Kentucky, in December 1975. By the time we reached lobby level, we all knew we had found lifetime friends…. These are not just 'Jon sermons'; these are 'Appleton sermons.' Each one comes from that inspired intellect of his…but he couldn't publish any of them until they earned the approval of Virginia's sensitive sermon-hearing skills. Here they are with our blessings and our prayer for God's blessings upon you as you read them."

Truett Gannon,
Pastor Emeritus,
Smoke Rise Baptist Church, Stone Mountain, Georgia

"Jon was invested in the people he cared for, as evidenced by personal touches, remembrances, and poems in services and ceremonies where he officiated. Jon's clever wit beautifully complemented his depth of character, intelligence, and integrity as he ministered to so very many people over the years. We consider ourselves to be truly blessed to be among those people."

Wayne and Mimi Dill,
First Baptist Church, Athens, Georgia

"Jon Appleton was an authentic, insightful, approachable, compassionate, prayerful, courageous, and committed pastor, and his sermons were the same way."

Tripp Martin,
Senior Pastor,
First Baptist Church, Auburn, Alabama

"Jon was a neighboring pastor with a poet's soul who welcomed me as a friend and colleague. When great sorrow came to our family, he cared for us and walked with us as he did for so many."

Jim Ross, Madison, Georgia

"Jon Appleton's sermons were good in his early years at First Baptist Athens. However, many were great in his later years."

Claude Williams Jr., Athens, Georgia

"For twenty-three years, Jon Appleton invited us into his mind and heart every Sunday with thoughtful sermons of God's love and grace. He challenged us to be open to surprise, mystery, and all of the unanswerable questions of our faith. His life and ministry were the sermons for us all. Now, those provocative thoughts are made available for each of us to glimpse into the personality and soul of one of our Baptist prophets."

Becky Matheny,
Pastor for Spiritual/Communal Development,
Lake Oconee Community Church, Greensboro, Georgia

www.ingramcontent.com/pod-product-compliance
Lightning Source LLC
Chambersburg PA
CBHW071005160426
43193CB00012B/1929